Portfolio Management

A practical guide

Portfolio Management

A practical guide

Association for Project Management

Association for Project Management
Ibis House, Regent Park
Summerleys Road, Princes Risborough
Buckinghamshire
HP27 9LE

© Association for Project Management 2019

First edition 2019

All rights reserved. No part of this publication may be reproduced, stored in a retrieval system, or transmitted, in any form or by any means, without the express permission in writing of the Association for Project Management. Within the UK exceptions are allowed in respect of any fair dealing for the purposes of research or private study, or criticism or review, as permitted under the Copyright, Designs and Patents Act, 1988, or in the case of reprographic reproduction in accordance with the terms of the licences issued by the Copyright Licensing Agency. Enquiries concerning reproduction outside these terms and in other countries should be sent to the Rights Department, Association for Project Management at the address above.

British Library Cataloguing in Publication Data is available.
Paperback ISBN: 978-1-903494-86-8
eISBN: 978-1-903494-87-5

Cover design by Fountainhead Creative Consultants
Typeset by RefineCatch Limited, Bungay, Suffolk
in 10/14pt Foundry Sans

Contents

List of figures and tables	vii
Preface	viii
About this guide	x
The authors	xii
Acknowledgements	xiii
Executive summary	xiv

1 Introduction to portfolio management — 1
- 1.1 Fundamentals of portfolio management — 1
- 1.2 How portfolio management contributes to organisations — 2
- 1.3 Signs your organisation might benefit from portfolio management — 3
- 1.4 Where does portfolio management fit within the organisation? — 4

2 Adopting portfolio management and the organisational context — 7
- 2.1 The strategic plan — 7
- 2.2 Portfolio governance — 10
- 2.3 Sponsorship and stakeholder engagement — 13
- 2.4 Portfolio management and management of risk — 14
- 2.5 Portfolio management ROI and benefits management — 18
- 2.6 Portfolio management of projects with different delivery methodologies — 19

3 Portfolio management core processes — 22
- 3.1 Construct and prioritise the portfolio — 22
- 3.2 Develop, monitor and control the portfolio — 28
- 3.3 Manage and deliver programmes and projects — 31
- 3.4 Review the portfolio — 31

Contents

	3.5	Reporting on the portfolio	33
	3.6	Assessing the performance of the portfolio	36
4	**Implementing portfolio management**		**40**
	4.1	Business drivers for portfolio management – understanding the business imperative	40
	4.2	Introducing portfolio management	42
	4.3	Establishing portfolio management	46
	4.4	Governance roles and relationship to organisational governance	48
	4.5	How to measure early success	53
	4.6	Challenges for portfolio management	53
5	**Recommended focus areas**		**58**
Appendix Summary roles and responsibilities			**60**
Glossary			**63**

List of figures and tables

Figures

1.1 How portfolio management contributes to business success — 3
1.2 Portfolio management framework – process overview — 5
2.1 Maturity of organisational approach to portfolio management – APM Portfolio SIG Survey — 10
2.2 Portfolio perspective — 12
2.3 Benefit risk model — 17
3.1 Construct and prioritise the portfolio — 23
3.2 A value score chart – benefit and cost comparison — 28
3.3 Example portfolio dependency map — 29
3.4 An example portfolio overview dashboard — 35
3.5 Portfolio performance assessment maturity model — 39
4.1 Strategy and portfolio alignment — 41
4.2 Centralised portfolio management — 50
4.3 Decentralised portfolio management — 51
4.4 Organisational skills levels — 55

Tables

1.1 Factors suggesting portfolio management might be beneficial — 4
4.1 RACI matrix for creating an effective portfolio environment — 52
A1 The roles involved in portfolio management, how they contribute and the value they deliver — 60

Preface

Many academic studies have been undertaken in portfolio management, but very few bring to life portfolio management in practice. This guide draws upon the experiences of more than 60 organisations, and shares good practice on how portfolio management can optimise projects to deliver business value.

All too many projects still fail to meet their targets, as outlined in the APM publication *Why do projects fail?*

> "Projects across industries and geographies struggle to meet the most basic targets. Five out of 10 technology projects, six out of 10 energy projects, seven out of 10 dams, nine out of 10 transport projects and 10 out of 10 Olympic Games do not meet their cost targets. This trend has been constant."[1]

No single approach to portfolio management should be viewed as a panacea. However, as we work towards a world where all projects succeed, we should not underestimate the value of portfolio management in helping all types of organisation to maximise their return on investment.

> A leading logistics company had at its core robust and disciplined portfolio management, with a portfolio made up of more than 100 projects, split into six programmes with 400 project professionals. At the heart of its success was improvement to portfolio management professionalism, supported by the APM, which over the prior seven years delivered £1bn in recurring annual benefit through the modernisation of the operation.

There are many competing factors that need to be pieced together to ensure the success of a portfolio. It's a bit like doing a jigsaw puzzle, it helps to have a clear picture of what you are working to construct. In this type of jigsaw, however,

---

[1] https://www.apm.org.uk/news/why-do-projects-fail/

Preface

you also have to recognise that the picture is constantly changing. The core pieces of the jigsaw tend to be quite uniform, and can be broadly categorised as customer, employee, shareholder, market and, frequently, regulators. But this is also a three-dimensional jigsaw – you have to build in short-term expectations and longer-term strategic goals, industrial relations, corporate governance, resources, funding and, in the case of research and development projects, certainty of outcome.

The balanced portfolio aligns outcomes to strategic goals, and the roadmap to those goals will vary. Like a satellite navigation system, which recalculates when it hits traffic, the portfolio manager has to respond to conditions to ensure the business goal is met.

Instrumental in making this work are a supportive sponsor (or more than one), an engaged, motivated and inspired portfolio team, and recognition that every change is different. Pull together all of these pieces and align to an appropriate governance mechanism and, although it can't be assured, success is at least achievable.

This guide identifies many of the ingredients for success in managing a portfolio of complex projects for positive business return. Every portfolio will need differing quantities of these ingredients, but we hope that this guide will at least help you determine the ingredients you need and set you on the road to portfolio management success.

Richard Moor
Head of portfolio, Royal Mail Letters and Network

About this guide

This guide illustrates how portfolio management is a key mechanism in enabling an organisation to optimise delivery of its strategic goals, maximising value, and do so in the required time frame.

The guide is designed to serve three main aims:

- to promote awareness of, and outline good practice in, portfolio management for the practising or developing portfolio manager or portfolio office manager. All organisations can learn from each other, but ultimately each needs to build its own version of portfolio management practice that addresses their own business need;
- to provide a benchmark for portfolio managers and the portfolio management community to assess their own organisation's maturity in the discipline;
- to stimulate new thinking and contribute to the development of portfolio management practice.

The guide is divided into four main sections:

Section 1: Introduction to portfolio management: This section explains what portfolio management comprises and why it is important to organisations. It outlines the kind of situations that an organisation might encounter where introducing portfolio management could bring significant benefits. This section concludes with examples of where portfolio management might fit within an organisation's structure; there is no 'one-size-fits-all' with portfolio management.

Section 2: Adopting portfolio management: This section deals with how portfolio management links to the existing organisational processes, such as strategic planning, stakeholder engagement, risk management, return on investment (ROI) and benefits. It also considers the different delivery methodologies. It shows how the purpose of portfolio management is to optimise delivery of the corporate strategy and goals, to ensure that all projects and programmes are directly contributing to achieving those goals.

Section 3: Portfolio management core processes: This section looks in depth at constructing the portfolio, including any business-as-usual (BAU) and other initiatives within its scope, and how it should be managed. It shows how to ensure that the portfolio is on track to deliver its benefits and the strategic goals, how to consider any adjustments, and mitigate portfolio-level risks. It includes the role of portfolio reviews (by the executive committee overseeing the portfolio), what to report and how to assess whether the portfolio comprises the most effective set of projects and programmes to achieve delivery of the strategic goals in the appropriate timeframe.

Section 4: Implementing portfolio management: This section illustrates how an organisation will need to clearly and unambiguously identify what will deliver value for them, and then adapt the practice of portfolio management to their needs. It suggests treating the introduction of portfolio management as a project in itself and shows how to deal with a number of key challenges, such as the cultural context. For example, organisations may need to put in place an executive-level sponsor to support the portfolio manager, with overall accountability for the success of the portfolio.

The APM Portfolio Management Specific Interest Group (SIG) has acquired many examples from experienced practitioners of good and best practice, collected at our SIG events, annual conferences and from our committee and members. We are pleased to be able to bring all of this together into a single guide and we hope it will serve our SIG members, and non-members, well.

We hope you enjoy reading the guide and that it contributes to your understanding of portfolio management, as well as that of your organisation, and so meets our SIG aim of helping organisations achieve their corporate strategy or strategic intent.

Please email any comments, questions or suggestions to: portfoliosig@apm.org.uk

Stephen Parrett and Steve Leary, co-chairs, APM Portfolio Management SIG, 2017–2018

Lynne Ratcliffe and Steve Leary, co-chairs, APM Portfolio Management SIG, 2018–2019

The authors

Mike Florence is an independent consultant and director at i-bizFLO.

Steve Leary is managing consultant at TCS and was co-chair of the Portfolio Management SIG in 2017–2018 and 2018–2019.

Richard Moor is the head of portfolio, Royal Mail Operations.

Marina Morillas Lara is a highly experienced programme and portfolio manager working in Spain.

Stephen Parrett has many years of consulting on portfolio management and related topics at executive level; he assisted in setting up the Portfolio Management SIG, was chair for five years and co-chair in 2017–2018.

Lynne Ratcliffe is the change governance and assurance consultant at the Yorkshire Building Society, and co-chair of the Portfolio Management SIG 2018–2019.

Adam Skinner is director of consulting at P2 Consulting Ltd.

Acknowledgements

This publication has been prepared by the APM Portfolio Management Specific Interest Group (SIG). The authors and reviewers are Adam Skinner, Anna Byrne, Lynne Ratcliffe, Marina Morillas Lara, Mike Florence, Nancy Olson, Petula Allison, Richard Moor, Stephen Parrett and Steve Leary.

The SIG is also grateful for the contributions from the rest of the SIG committee for 2017–2018 and 2018–2019: Dwain Morgan, Gemma Parker, Gina Parkin, Paul Morgan, Peter Glynne, Simon Darby, Tanya Durlen and Tony Whitmore, and the external reviewers John Bennett, Anna Gray, Martin Samphire, Neil White, Sarah Harris and Andrew Schuster.

We would like to acknowledge our SIG members and guest speakers who contributed through debate, discussion and case-study presentations.

Executive summary

Mature portfolio management practices can deliver greater value to an organisation through more predictable and more efficient achievement of its strategic goals. It does this by helping to guide the board to invest money and resources in the most appropriate projects and programmes in the context of their strategic goals.

Key to the success of portfolio management is the relationship between strategy and implementation, with strong alignment between the organisation's strategic goals and those of the portfolio. For this reason, portfolio management should be seen as an integral part of the business planning, delivery and benefits realisation cycle.

There are many different approaches to portfolio management, and the one adopted will depend on the needs and context of your organisation. The one thing all approaches have in common is the importance of engaging stakeholders – particularly the senior executives, who are by definition the sponsors of the strategic portfolio.

Portfolio management contributes to organisations in many crucial ways:

- **Provides a focal point for strategic goals**. Portfolio management should be complementary to the overall management of the organisation; it is not an additional bureaucracy. The board sets the vision for the organisation, the corporate mission and the strategic goals, and how they expect those goals to be achieved. Without clearly defined organisation goals, the portfolio helping to achieve them cannot succeed. Decisions to start, stop and continue projects are based on these goals, and only these goals.
- **Ensures the prioritisation of the goals, with prioritisation rules for projects and programmes that are clear and unambiguous**. Clearly defined and prioritised goals are essential for decision making at a portfolio level, which then leads to more transparent and realistic decisions. Portfolio management helps executives to articulate the prioritisation criteria which contributes to improved decision making. For example, if all goals are 'high priority' then in reality none are, and decisions will be taken on other factors.

Executive summary

- **Helps ensure the whole board and executives are fully behind the approach, are sponsoring the portfolio and are actively championing portfolio management and empowering a capable team.** Ideally, everyone from the very top, through middle and junior management of the organisation needs to champion the strategy and the portfolio to ensure 'buy in' from the whole workforce to a structured portfolio management approach. An honest and collaborative style will build and engender trust within the management team across the portfolio and organisation.
- **Provides the capability to assess all key change factors.** It takes into account the constraints of opportunity, threat, resource availability, affordability, customer impact and the organisation's capacity to absorb and manage change. In doing this, it enables the managing of projects and programmes at a collective level, through effective corporate governance, engagement of key stakeholders, adherence to key processes and the optimisation of limited resources and dependencies.
- **Considers in-flight projects and programmes and business as usual (BAU) in the same way and ensure full alignment to the strategic goals.** Portfolio management should always aim to balance competing demands from within and outside the scope of the portfolio to ensure business success. Decisions taken on balancing BAU and change, and allocation of resources must be measured against those same strategic goals. Effective portfolio management is a collaborative partnership across the organisation. The core message is to prioritise and keep prioritising throughout the portfolio life.
- **Ensures 'tactical' projects contribute to the strategic goals – if they don't, don't do them**. There will always be a place for tactical projects within a portfolio, but they all need to take the organisation in the right direction towards one (or more) of its strategic goals. Tactical projects take finite resources away from others delivering the strategic objectives, usually for immediate support to a short-term goal. Questions need to be asked as to whether the portfolio is correctly balanced and if the organisation really needs to do a project or piece of work. If the work is critical, ensure it doesn't render any other outcome impossible.
- **Embeds portfolio governance into the organisation's controls and makes it robust**. Additional governance is unnecessary provided an organisation has mature controls where portfolio governance can be aligned with the business planning and decision-making processes ensuring seamless

Executive summary

delivery. If implementing for the first time, it is important to make sure portfolio management is fully integrated with organisational processes.

- **Critically assesses what information is really needed to make portfolio decisions**. At C-suite level, the information provided, whether at a project, programme or the portfolio itself, needs to be 'lead' information and 'just enough' (i.e. enough information but no more) to make a decision, and always be directly related to achievement of the strategic goals. To ensure clarity and transparency of decision making, the board need to have just the right level of information to make decisions. As decisions need to be made on what will happen in the future, meaningful lead metrics, such as goal alignment, benefit and risk, are essential.
- **Provides the means to be consistent and fair across the portfolio, irrespective of the programme or project sponsor's influence.** For example, although they may be hard to challenge, 'pet' projects do not always align to the strategic goals and can divert valuable resources. Individual sponsors may support projects for many reasons, and will have their biases; these need to be understood. Through having a clear and transparent process the influence of such biases and internal politics should be minimised.

The true value of portfolio management is to help keep the organisation focussed on achieving the strategic goals, thereby delivering them in a timely fashion. It all too often takes a 'burning platform' to focus minds and draw enough senior stakeholder interest and resources to make an organisation fully adopt portfolio management. Ultimately the question is: given the resources and capabilities available and the inherent uncertainty in the projects and programmes, can the organisation meet its strategic objectives with the 'portfolio' it currently has?

If not, effective portfolio management is likely to be the answer. This guide will show how portfolio management can help, from its establishment through to effective management of a portfolio, realisation of the benefits and achievement of the strategic goals.

1

Introduction to portfolio management

1.1 Fundamentals of portfolio management

The seventh edition of the *APM Body of Knowledge* defines portfolio management as: *"the selection, prioritisation and control of an organisation's projects and programmes in line with its strategic objectives and capacity to deliver."*

Other definitions incorporate the same themes of prioritisation, control and organisation. The key message is that portfolio management has to be fully integrated into the business planning and management cycle; it should be considered part of routine, regular governance.

There are many different approaches to portfolio management, and the one adopted will depend on the needs and context of the organisation. No two portfolios are the same, every organisation's culture is different, and maturity levels vary.

The one thing all the approaches have in common is the importance of engaging stakeholders, and particularly the senior executives who are by definition the sponsors of the strategic portfolio. Portfolio management operates at the strategic level of an organisation, and without strategic stakeholder support it will not work as well as it could.

Against this backdrop, there are a number of key threads that help ensure that maximum value is delivered for the organisation through portfolio management. Think of these as 'golden rules' for successful portfolio management.

For the purpose of this guide an initiative can be a project, programme or portfolio. It is a set of activities or work packages that needs to be completed to achieve a business objective or goal.

Portfolio management can be implemented in a business area, business unit or at a functional level. However, to achieve maximum benefit, it should ideally be implemented at an enterprise level. Many organisations go through a maturation of portfolio management practices with functions or divisions, e.g. IT might use it within their domain and, once the benefits are recognised, it then becomes easier to implement at an organisational level.

Portfolio Management

In the public sector, portfolio management can be used across multiple organisations to support systems. A typical example is in health and social care, where there has been the need to find cost savings as well as provide more integrated services to the public:

> Some of the more advanced health and social care systems are now using a form of portfolio management to deliver transformation across multiple organisations. A board is established with the CEOs of the organisations that make up the agreed geographical area; this would typically include the hospital trusts, primary care organisations, local authorities and mental health trusts. They establish a portfolio of programmes and projects, supported by business-as-usual, to bring improvements in the outcomes for patients, clients and communities. These types of portfolio usually have an element of cost saving attached to them, ensuring that they are prioritising those projects and programmes that bring about better outcomes at lower cost. This can be achieved by removing duplication, creating efficiencies from economies of scale, being more able to afford and embrace new technologies and facilitating the establishment of specific patient pathways.

1.2 How portfolio management contributes to organisations

Portfolio management helps guide the board to invest money and resources in the 'right' projects and programmes in the context of their strategic goals. This enables organisations to better react to changes within the marketplace, as well as achieve the goals set by the executives.

It also takes into account the constraints of opportunity, threat, resource availability, affordability, customer impact and the organisation's capacity to absorb and manage change through application of key, consistent processes.

Finally, it enables the managing of projects and programmes at a collective level, through effective governance, engagement of key stakeholders, adherence to key processes and the optimisation of limited resources and dependencies.

As identified through the portfolio management specific interest group conferences, there are multiple values, added benefits and improved outcomes

Introduction to portfolio management

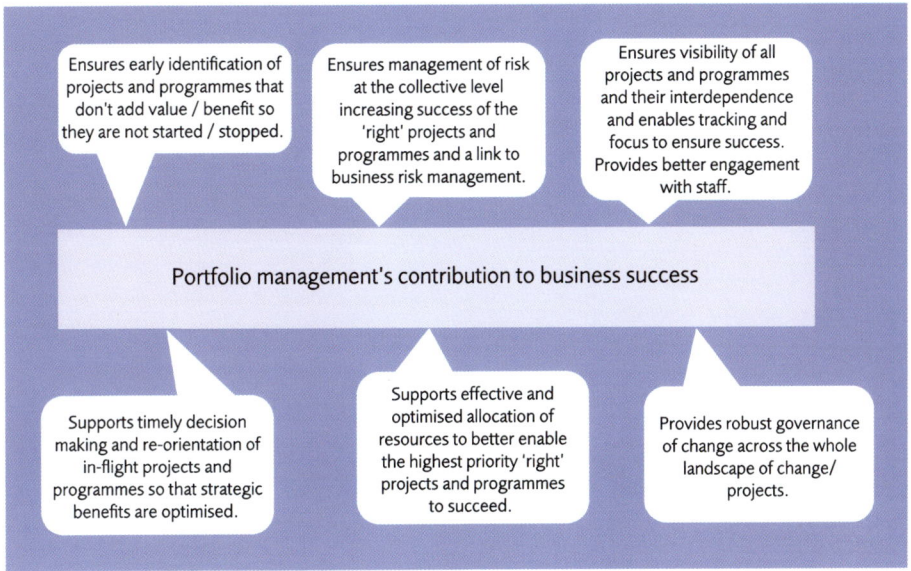

Figure 1.1 How portfolio management contributes to business success

when portfolio management is implemented and properly executed. Some of those are explained in the executive summary.

Case studies of portfolio management across multiple organisations have identified a number of ways in which portfolio management contributes to the project management context and success – summarised in Figure 1.1.

1.3 Signs your organisation might benefit from portfolio management

It often takes a 'burning platform' to focus minds and draw enough senior stakeholder interest and resources to make an organisation fully adopt portfolio management. The APM thought leadership publication, *Recognising the Need to Change: Six telling signs* has identified six 'classic symptoms' that organisations exhibit, which tend to drive these challenging moments. When building a case for portfolio management, it is helpful to look out for these.

Ultimately, the question to answer is: given the resources and capabilities available and the inherent uncertainty in the projects and programmes, can the organisation meet its strategic objectives with the portfolio it currently has? If not, effective portfolio management may be the answer.

Portfolio Management

	Sign	Impact
1	Lack of coordination or alignment to business strategy	Individual behaviours, organisational ways of working and external drivers are factors preventing the ability to align change to the organisation's overall priorities
2	Scope of programmes not clear or overlapping	Individual programmes are not clear or are overlapping in scope and require a holistic review and restructure to minimise critical interdependencies. Vested interest, along with overly possessive executive ownership of programmes and a lack of a strong chief executive or equivalent senior leader, are preventing this
3	Behaviours that 'tell a story'	Senior leaders are ignoring the impact of executive stress and negative behaviours during periods of intense or imposed change
4	Inability to quickly reprioritise in response to changing circumstances	The organisation cannot easily reprioritise its change. This is a primary signal highlighting the need for effective portfolio management
5	Inability to balance resources with projects and programmes	The organisation has far more opportunities than resources to deliver them – and is incapable of making choices. There are disparate/competing views of project priorities, leading to very different allocations of resource across functions in an organisation
6	Ineffective communication on change and organisational priorities	There are often conflicting or mixed messages within change communications, leading to a reliance on hearsay and rumour. Communication failures are leading to reputational damage both inside and outside the organisation

Table 1.1 Factors suggesting portfolio management might be beneficial

1.4 Where does portfolio management fit within the organisation?

Portfolio management should not be considered in isolation, but as a core part of the business planning and delivery process. Figure 1.2 shows the business cycle of processes from vision through to achievement of the goals and delivery to the strategy. It will be an iterative and continuing process and, depending on the industry, each cycle may span several years.

The vision, corporate goals and strategy need to be defined and communicated clearly and unambiguously through the organisation. This includes the metrics

Introduction to portfolio management

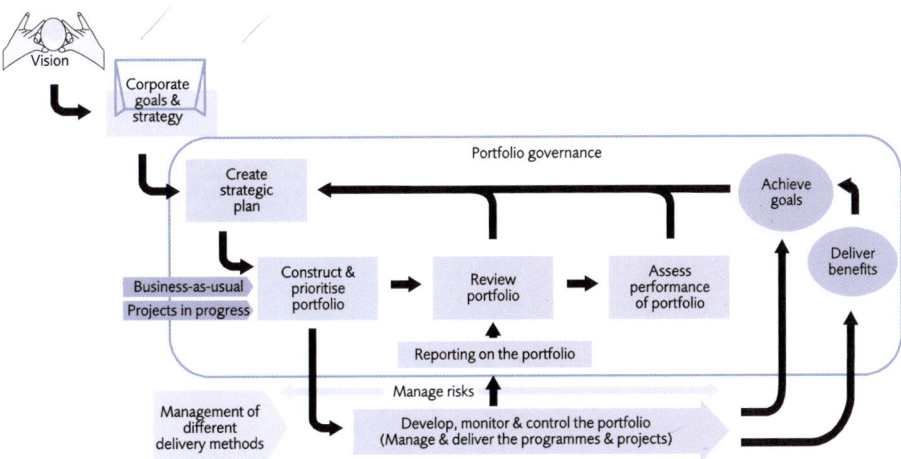

Figure 1.2 Portfolio management framework – process overview

that will be used, so we know when we've achieved those strategic goals, and the priority of these goals in relation to each other. Portfolio management then works out how to deliver these goals via programmes and projects.

The portfolio (or portfolios) is/are then constructed to deliver these goals, considering existing projects and programmes and BAU or operations, by ranking the initiatives according to the priorities set by the board, i.e. the priorities of the goals. The prioritised projects and programmes are authorised and funded within the financial constraints.

Developing the portfolio includes managing the investment and initiatives through the project and programme governance to optimise delivery of the goals and the ROI or other criteria.

Reporting at a portfolio level should be just enough (and no more) to enable the portfolio reviewers to make decisions on what starts, what stops, and which resources can be better utilised by reallocating to different projects. Feedback from benefits realised against the benefits planned, delivery performance and capability inform current and future investment decisions. Emerging risks and opportunities feed into the portfolio review and influence the decisions taken. More detail can be found in section 3.5.

Assessing the overall business performance against the strategic goals enables the organisation to evaluate how it is reacting to changes, including external pressures and new challenges, and to measure whether the portfolio is delivering

Portfolio Management

to expectations. It also enables the improvement and evolution of the management of internal shared resources and processes that are not owned by projects but upon which they depend, e.g. procurement, legal, employee relations and recruitment.

The business and benefits performance metrics need to be clearly defined to support the decisions to be made – what information is required to make decisions to stop, start or continue projects or programmes, or to reallocate resources? The sole purpose of the portfolio is to deliver the business strategy, without compromising BAU to the extent that you put the future state at risk. As such, it should be embedded in the regular governance cycles.

2

Adopting portfolio management and the organisational context

This section deals with how portfolio management links to the organisational processes such as strategic planning, stakeholder engagement, risk management, ROI and benefits. It also considers the different delivery methodologies. Figure 1.2 provides a framework and overview of the processes.

Section 3 addresses the core processes that are more specific to portfolio management.

2.1 The strategic plan

The board sets the vision for the organisation, the corporate mission and the strategic goals, and how they expect those goals to be achieved. Depending on the organisation's structure, these may be devolved to a divisional level, or to a group of business areas or business units.

This strategic planning process defines what is required and determines the high-level plan to meet the targets set by the board, i.e. the goals and strategy. The portfolio management team works closely with the strategy group (or equivalent), plus the executives and business area directors and managers within the organisation, to develop the portfolio plan to achieve those goals.

2.1.1 Goals and objectives

The corporate goals need to be framed with a clear focus on the changes required, and should include targets and metrics.

- The goals and strategy drive the changes. The task of the portfolio manager/ function is to work with the management and planning teams to ensure that goals and objectives and the required strategies are understood and can be achieved.

Portfolio Management

- The portfolio represents the organisational changes necessary to meet the strategic goals, and hence will include how various programmes, projects, and business unit plans contribute to those goals.

Portfolio management is an integral part of the strategic planning process and supports the 'how' of strategic delivery and implementation through such things as modelling possible portfolio outcomes to provide various forward views for consideration. These models will include current, in-flight projects as well as new contenders, and should provide views on the potential impact on business-as-usual (BAU) or operational processes that will be already in place and delivering.

Commercial considerations will determine the level of investment and flexibility for a given period, and hence will influence how soon the goals might be achieved.

2.1.2 Process and organisational alignment and embedding

The portfolio will be managed to meet the strategic goals and optimise the overall ROI and benefits, and therefore will ensure that the objectives of the business units' and functions' projects and programmes are directly contributing to, and fully aligned with, those strategic goals. The projects and programmes will themselves be planned and managed in the usual way using 'standard' project and programme management and controls. Although the portfolio management function does not manage the individual projects and programmes, it will set the priorities and influence areas such as resource allocation and timeline planning.

The overall planning process also considers BAU or operational plans – i.e. the total investment (revenue and capital) that the organisation is making.

Budget planning and portfolio planning processes are often iterative, looking at business demand, capability, internal and external risks and pressures and funding availability. A high-level portfolio plan can help determine what can realistically be achieved and identify the resources and skills required. As options are reviewed and agreed the portfolio and associated budgets can be set, together with outline budgets for subsequent periods and the lifetimes of the projects and programmes. The amount of change also needs to be considered so that the business can absorb the planned changes while continuing to operate.

An annual cycle is unlikely to be frequent enough for the portfolio reviews and several organisations have moved to a six-monthly or quarterly cycle. Such reviews may also be triggered by market or other major events and lead to re-alignment of investment and resources outside the 'normal' financial and portfolio planning cycles.

Adopting portfolio management and the organisational context

It is critical, however, that the portfolio governance is embedded into the overall organisational governance, and this may influence the frequency of portfolio reviews. The reviews should be aligned so that there will be a 'cadence' of reviews at the project, programme, portfolio and board level.

2.1.3 Prioritisation of the corporate strategic goals

The strategic goals that have been set should be assigned a priority in relation to each other, and this will be determined by the overall corporate strategic priorities. This will equally apply where divisions/business units have agreed their own goals. Decisions made at portfolio reviews will be informed/directed by the prioritisation of these goals as set by the board.

All the board members need to be fully committed and accept collective responsibility for the prioritisation and weighting, as well as for the goals themselves.

To achieve a portfolio that stays in balance, it is necessary to plan in line with the timescales of the strategic objectives, and potentially beyond, and update regularly. Rather than set a fixed portfolio (e.g. for the plan year) it becomes a 'rolling portfolio' with a longer strategic horizon, linked to appropriate periodic review points.

The output of this process is likely to include:

- agreed strategic goals and priorities;
- a strategic plan;
- overall budget limits;
- high-level schedule, with key high-level milestones;
- a set of high-level portfolio goals and objectives. These may be determined for each business area, or group of business areas, outlining the major programmes and major projects (or groups of projects) that will be required, including in-flight projects and associated BAU or operational targets.

The process would initiate programme definition phases and outline project briefs for new work, and all become part of portfolio construction and prioritisation (PC&P). In most organisations, PC&P will have started during the initial planning process and will conclude in an agreed portfolio aligned with the final set of organisational business goals and plans.

Portfolio Management

2.2 Portfolio governance

The overall process was summarised in section 1, figure 1.2. The diagram shows the key processes within the overall framework. The governance cycle includes construction and prioritisation of the portfolio, review, reporting, and assessing the performance of the portfolio. These will be described in more detail in section 3.

2.2.1 Definition and purpose, and relationship to organisational governance

The board (or equivalent) has accountability for, and sits at the apex of, the organisation's governance and is accountable for effective management of the enterprise-wide portfolio.

Portfolio governance ensures that the overall investment is optimised. It says *what* must be done and *why* in terms of the strategic plan and goals, and ideally *by when* the objectives need to be achieved. However, it is for the programmes and projects to work out *how* and *when* it is achievable, develop the detail of *why* into the business case and plan the *where* and *who*. In doing this, it draws upon the organisation's experience of managing and delivering change to develop the optimal schedule and sequence for the portfolio.

There are diverse levels of maturity of portfolio management and governance, as illustrated by the results of an APM Portfolio Management SIG survey:

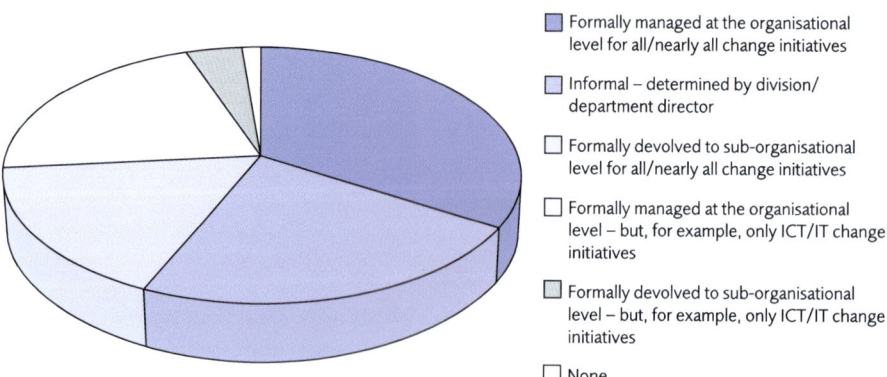

Figure 2.1 Maturity of organisational approach to portfolio management – APM Portfolio SIG survey

The survey indicates that only a third of organisations manage their change initiatives through a formal portfolio management and governance mechanism; the other two-thirds having varying degrees of portfolio management, indicating lower levels of capability maturity.

2.2.2 Governance cycle

Portfolio governance is part of the organisation's overall decision-making model and needs to be fully embedded into the organisation's top-level governance, i.e. the board meetings, executive reviews of strategic performance and regular management meetings. The introduction of portfolio management should add minimal levels of bureaucracy, but it often changes the focus of the governance and management information (MI) from largely historical reporting to 'lead' indicators, with a horizon of maybe three months, six months or longer, depending on the industry and organisation. It generally necessitates a thorough review and overhaul of the existing governance arrangements and management meetings.

Any activity that takes portfolio resources would be subject to portfolio governance, e.g. a study to gain information or test a technology, a market survey, a delivery initiative, a one-off activity or a fact-finding mission.

The construction, prioritisation and development of the portfolio can be broken down into sub-processes that represent the life cycle of an individual programme or project.

The prioritisation is typically a weighted assessment of strategy contribution, benefits expected, overall project risk or achievability, and whole life cost, i.e. the strategy contribution and the business case. Benefits would normally be risk adjusted. The governance cycle including governance arrangements and prioritisation process is discussed in more detail in section 3.

2.2.3 Portfolio perspective

As well as the programme, project or initiative life cycle, from portfolio entry to actual benefits and contribution to the strategic goal, portfolio management governance looks *across* the portfolio. The portfolio governance board assesses whether the initiatives are contributing to achieving the strategic goals and whether they represent the optimum investment for the organisation. This is measured in terms of 'to go' costs and the contribution to meeting the strategy. If the strategy can be achieved quicker or more effectively by reallocating resources to other initiatives, then this should be done.

Portfolio Management

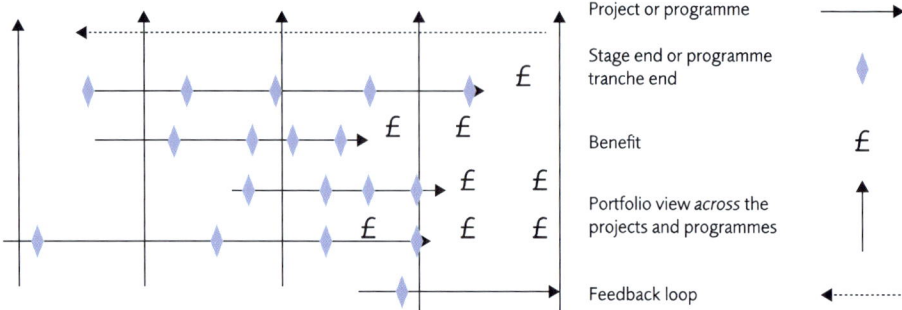

Figure 2.2 Portfolio perspective

The diagram above represents projects and programmes (horizontal lines) with stage gates or tranche ends (diamonds). Benefits are represented by £s.

The dotted horizontal line from right to left at the top represents the feedback from delivery and benefits to inform the portfolio process. The x-axis represents time.

Portfolio governance looks across the projects and programmes, the vertical arrows, and makes decisions on what should be stopped, what should be started and whether resources need to be reassigned to achieve the overall strategic goals and optimise the ROI and benefit, considering the levels of risk.

Frequently, tactical initiatives are requested. The organisation or business unit strategy sets the criteria for assessment of these. This strategy might include, for example, that 60 per cent of the change budget is to be spent on 'major' initiatives delivering key strategic goals, and 40 per cent is for tactical initiatives that give an ROI of at least 10 to 1 and contribute to the strategic goals. These criteria will be individual to each organisation and the organisation's priorities, and will need to balance the investment in overall change with the investment in BAU. This balance and the criteria would be set and managed by the portfolio manager, or portfolio executive, in line with the strategic goals set by the board (see section 2.1.1). The criteria need to be clear and unambiguous, and there may be a hierarchy of criteria.

One useful measure of the effectiveness of the governance is the number, or value, of projects or programmes each year that get stopped in flight as they no longer represent the best use of resources. This will vary by industry and organisation. If very few are stopped, the effectiveness of the portfolio governance and review processes may need to be questioned. However, as portfolio management matures, fewer projects and programmes are likely to be stopped, as portfolio management ensures that initiatives meet tough criteria before they start, and rapid corrective action can be taken on in-flight projects.

2.3 Sponsorship and stakeholder engagement

The APM definition of a sponsor is as follows:

> "A critical role as part of the governance board of any project, programme or portfolio. The sponsor is accountable for ensuring that the work is governed effectively and delivers the objectives that meet identified needs."

The sponsor of the programme or project owns the business case. There must be a close relationship between the sponsor, the project or programme manager, and the portfolio manager, to ensure that each project or programme continues to be aligned with strategy. Will the initiative deliver the defined outputs and benefits, and so contribute to achieving the strategic goals? If it is no longer aligned to the strategy, e.g. the strategy has changed, or if the value of predicted benefits no longer supports the business case, the sponsor and project manager must work with the portfolio manager, either to close the programme or project or to realign it and then re-prioritise it according to the prioritisation rules.

At the executive level, portfolio management as a way of working must be fully and actively supported. There is no place for 'pet projects' – criteria for portfolio entry and prioritisation must be clear, unambiguous and rigorously applied. If this does not happen, the process will be undermined and the investment not optimal. However, in practice, it may initially be difficult to gain full support for portfolio management, and experience indicates that support for it develops and is embedded over a number of years as its value becomes clearer. It is therefore critical to allow adequate time for the processes to be embedded and to evolve. The time needed will depend on the organisation's culture, the degree of executive alignment and encouragement, and whether the people involved work as a team or as a group of individuals with slightly differing agendas. In people terms, this needs careful handing – as people generally have an emotional attachment to initiatives they have been working on – as well as managing the communications within the business. Conference presentations by organisations from both the public and private sectors have consistently indicated that it takes 18 months to two years to fully embed portfolio management.

Some organisations have successfully introduced portfolio management by treating it as a change programme in itself. Selling the idea and continually communicating and demonstrating the value and benefits of portfolio management are key to getting buy-in, as illustrated in the example below. This is discussed further in section 4.

> The successful transformation of a major corporation's operation, methods, systems, infrastructure and automation was a major enabler to securing the future of the company. At the heart of this success was strong sponsorship, led from the very top of the organisation by the CEO, the executive team and the board. This included ensuring that all managers had a full line of sight to the key deliverables of the transformation programme. Sponsors led from the front, providing simple messaging in a knowledgeable and hands-on manner. Portfolio governance was also underpinned by sponsors working actively alongside their project and programme team in support of successful delivery to time, cost and quality. The effective role of the sponsors was key and remains a major ingredient to the continued success of this corporation's change journey.

2.4 Portfolio management and management of risk

One of the considerations is maintaining the overall risk profile across the portfolio, i.e. balancing the number of high-risk and potentially high-benefit projects with lower-risk and lower-benefit projects. The portfolio governance board needs to ensure the overall risk profile remains in line with the risk strategy, or risk appetite, of the organisation, as set by the board. This will differ by industry.

Projects and programmes have their own risk management mechanisms; portfolio risk management does not sit 'above' that or interfere with that mechanism. It is a separate (but linked) process.

Portfolio risk management has the following five aims:

1. Assessing and mitigating risks that may impact the strategic goals, whether internal or external to the organisation, system, function etc.

Adopting portfolio management and the organisational context

2. Meeting the portfolio risk profile agreed with the board, or recommending changing the risk profile.
3. Establishing a model for assessing overall project or programme complexity and therefore likelihood of success (or level of risk). A valuable tool provided by the APM is the competency framework which assesses projects as complex rather than complicated.
4. Identifying systemic risks, i.e. those risks that are apparent in several projects or programmes, and then coordinating the response to these systemic risks.
5. Ensuring project and programme risks are assessed and managed in a consistent way.

The fifth aim is met by having standard processes and procedures for risk identification, evaluation, assessment, review and escalation. The portfolio is accountable for ensuring that the processes and procedures and governance are consistent, although not necessarily the same, so comparisons can be made within the portfolio. This will include consistent templates, ways of defining risks, assessment and evaluation and mitigating actions. The projects and programmes then manage within this consistent governance.

Common or systemic risks that are identified in several projects are likely to need a coordinated treatment. The portfolio management team (or equivalent) therefore has to scan the project and programme risks, identify what appear to be similar risks, and then work with the individual project managers and the portfolio manager to determine whether the factors are common, and if so, how best to address them. This could be, for example, by one of the project managers taking the lead and defining and taking mitigating action on behalf of several projects affected by the risk.

> A global organisation noted that at the portfolio review several projects were showing a 'red' status against risk. On examination, these were due to the risk of an infrastructure item and service from a particular supplier not being delivered on time. Further investigation revealed that the supplier's capacity was limited and that the project requests were not being confirmed early enough to allow a capacity increase. Working with the supplier and improving the demand forecast enabled these risks to be reduced and largely eliminated.

Portfolio Management

External factors, e.g. market shift, competitive action, new regulations, or internal changes such as a change of business direction, may lead to risks on the projects and/or programmes or on the whole portfolio. Techniques such as 'PESTLIED' (political, economic, social, technological, legal, international, environmental and demographic) can assist in identifying these risks, and it is then for the organisation to decide the likelihood and impact, and what mitigating actions to take. These broader risks would be managed at a portfolio or possibly programme level, and might, for example, involve the CEO engaging with the government or a regulatory body.

In addition to individual risks associated with a programme or project, there needs to be an assessment of the likelihood of successful delivery; and overall risk to that programme or project, in terms of its ability to deliver. This may be based on an assessment of the complexity of the project and programme, on the thinking that the greater the complexity, the higher the risk of not delivering. This is different from the individual risks within a project or programme.

Several factors will influence the assessment of overall risk, and there are a number of models available. Most of these take into consideration factors such as:

- clarity of requirements;
- technology risk (e.g. higher risk with new or untried technology);
- lack of availability of skills, particularly critical skills, and resources. This may include vendor resource;
- complexity of the management of the stakeholders – the overall risk increases with the number of key stakeholders, taking into consideration whether they are co-located or dispersed, largely supportive or not;
- ease or difficulty of implementation, for example organisational experience – have we done this before?
- too much change and the risk to implementation and realising the benefits increases.

Adopting portfolio management and the organisational context

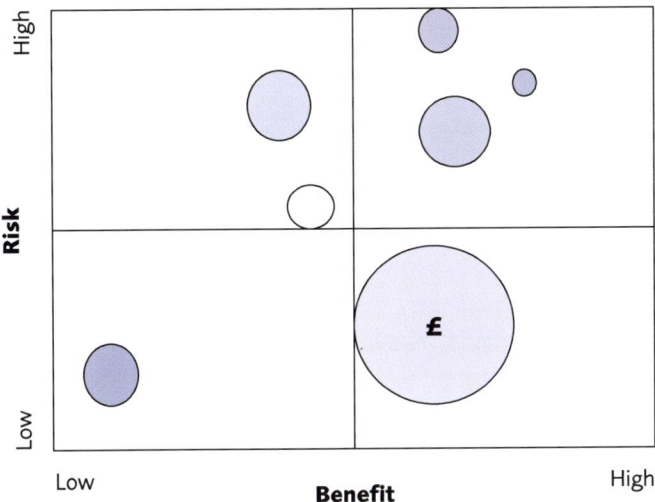

Figure 2.3 Benefit risk model

A consistent model can be applied to the projects and programmes to produce a four-box diagram.

This simple example shows projects delivering on a benefits scale from low to high, and with a risk (or complexity) scale from low to high, with the size of the 'bubble' proportionate to the investment cost.

A risk profile, or 'risk appetite', set by the organisation might be that no more than 25 per cent of its projects should be high-risk. In this example the portfolio manager would be expected to work with the project manager and sponsor to 'move' some of these projects to a lower-risk position. This could be by reducing the scope, bringing in specialist suppliers at additional expense who are familiar with the technology, or breaking the project up and finding different solutions to riskier parts of it. This overall risk assessment of each project is an element of the prioritisation evaluation.

> A UK retailer links its portfolio-level risk management process to the corporate-level risk management function. This ensures that significant portfolio risks are made visible at the board level in conjunction with other corporate-level risks, e.g. business continuity. It also enables the company to receive support or valuable resources from the board, if it is required to help mitigate these risks.

2.5 Portfolio management ROI and benefits management

The purpose of portfolio management (and of many other organisational functions) is to optimise delivery of the corporate strategy and goals. It asks 'Are all projects and programmes directly contributing to achieving the goals?'.

It may be advantageous to reallocate resources from a particular project, which may have a good business case, to a project with a less-attractive business case, but in so doing enable a key component of a corporate goal to be met earlier. This has to be balanced with other components of the corporate goal – but that's the key role of the portfolio manager and the board, balancing the portfolio to achieve the goals and optimise return. There will be conflicting pressures that the board, sponsors and portfolio manager will need to resolve. The portfolio represents the optimum investment by the organisation to meet its strategic goals. There will be many different portfolio options, i.e. different mixes of projects and programmes and possibly BAU, with varying degrees of risk and benefit. The 'efficient frontier', originally developed for financial portfolios, is a modern portfolio technique that compares the risk and return for the various options, and enables the selection of the best return, given the risk appetite of the organisation.

> A large bank had publicly set its strategy on a single, specific goal in a defined timescale. No project or programme, irrespective of the benefits or business case, was approved if it didn't directly and specifically contribute to meeting that goal. The rule was applied rigorously and over-rode any other benefits. They achieved their stated goal on schedule.

Project or programme governance optimises the particular project or programme outcome. Portfolio governance, however, optimises the overall investment outcome. This includes optimising the ROI and, as part of that, maximising the benefits at a portfolio level, i.e. across the portfolio, not just by project or programme.

Benefits are managed at the project and programme level, but are usually realised and tracked after the programme or project has been completed. This benefits tracking is a key input to the portfolio management process, as it informs decision making. It may be that, for example, benefits for a particular geographic region, or for a particular business area, are routinely over- or understated in the business cases. Initiatives for that region or business area can therefore be reviewed in the light of this, and this may affect their prioritisation within the portfolio.

The optimum ROI and benefits across a portfolio will not just be the sum of those of the individual projects and programmes. The aim is to balance the risk-adjusted benefits, the investment, and the risk to meet the strategic goals, and then to optimise return. Portfolio management largely eliminates double-counting of benefits. The regular portfolio reviews reprioritise the individual projects and programmes where needed, and this prioritisation is a key to achieving the strategic goals and optimising the portfolio ROI and benefits.

Portfolio management, when applied effectively, significantly increases the likelihood of the business achieving its strategic goals. It provides early learning within the organisation, and responsiveness when things go off track.

2.6 Portfolio management of projects with different delivery methodologies

Many portfolio management styles adopt a linear ('waterfall'-style) approach to delivery of their projects and programmes. This assumes that all projects are supported by a business case detailing cost, schedule and benefits to varying degrees of confidence, and that prioritisation and reprioritisation can be based on progress and outlook towards those benefits. In the current environment, however, very few organisations operate purely linear delivery, with the vast majority using a combination of linear, iterative ('agile'-based) and hybrid, methodologies. The selection of delivery method is a programme or project governance decision, and the most appropriate method should be selected to meet the objectives of the project. The portfolio manager needs to understand the different methodologies being applied within their portfolio and the implications of these for the portfolio management approach.

It is a common misconception that agile methodologies do not involve 'planning' or 'assurance'. However, both these critical functions do have a different flavour when it comes to agile methodologies. At their core they embrace the inherent uncertainty of delivering change and look to benefit from this uncertainty by focusing on the minimum viable product (the most basic product with the minimum number of features that allow initial testing with early adopters), and the cost of opportunities to improve on that.

Portfolio Management

2.6.1 Comparing linear (waterfall) and iterative (agile) projects

One approach to managing this difference at the portfolio level is to ignore it and insist that all projects, no matter the delivery approach, work to a common set of programme/project stages or milestones and submit a standardised business case from which to extract costs and benefits. In other words, extrapolating the data to a level that can be compared. This is not recommended, as trying to 'balance' the elements within the portfolio without taking into account the nuances of those different projects will mean that the portfolio is likely to favour one delivery approach over another, or fail to understand the risks of one approach over another.

2.6.2 Managing the hybrid or bi-modal portfolio

The specific approach to managing a hybrid, or bi-modal, portfolio will depend on the delivery methodologies used. However, there are generally several standard areas to be wary of:

1) Managing the level of certainty – experience suggests linear business cases tend to assert cost/benefit/time but are over-optimistic about how accurate these measures are. Properly delivered agile methodologies should have far more confidence about the time and cost elements of their business cases than linear ('waterfall') methodologies but can only commit to the 'minimum viable product' (MVP) benefits (where the agile teams have a good level of maturity). Benefits beyond the MVP would be identified during iteration. The portfolio level must be sensitive to this and should be willing to allocate a likely benefit above the MVP benefit, or risk the iterative business case consistently looking poorer than its linear equivalent.
2) Supporting iteration – portfolio analysis is aided by large programmes with benefits that can be predicted to drop ideally once a year to tie into the annual life cycle. Agile methodologies tend to iterate towards a solution, leading to larger numbers of deployments but each growing the benefits of the project. To be effective, the portfolio management approach must be granular enough to understand the value of this ongoing and iterative growth of benefit as opposed to a single major drop.
3) Understanding the role of the stakeholder – most agile methodologies require very active engagement with stakeholders, who will identify the most valuable benefits to be developed as the projects and programmes progress. This

means that both the size and, more challengingly, the nature of the benefits can change fairly fluidly, beyond the MVP level, as the project adapts. This can make it particularly challenging to group the benefits of a particular project into the traditional categories/value streams that portfolio management tends to require (e.g. customer value, efficiency, regulatory requirement). The portfolio manager must either work to reduce 'benefit value' to a single comparable measure (such as cost), or adopt a system that allows regular and rapid reassessment of the benefits likely to be delivered by all projects.

4) For true portfolio optimisation, involving factoring in the 'risk to delivery' of a particular project, the fundamentally different risk profiles of the different delivery methodologies need to be understood – for instance, linear projects should have a reducing delivery risk profile with far greater uncertainty at the beginning, whereas agile methodology projects should maintain a lower but fairly constant risk profile, due to the iterative nature of their development and that each 'stage' goes through design/build/test.

In summary, the different approaches need to be understood and considered in their own right before agreeing the minimum level of reporting and information that is required. Understand what your portfolio management approach needs to deliver in terms of value, then work out where that information can be drawn from in the different methodologies. Portfolio management needs to take into account all the different methodologies available to project managers.

3

Portfolio management core processes

Portfolio management directs and manages the prioritisation of project investment to deliver the corporate goals and strategy. It should become a continuous activity, embedded within the organisation's governance and day-to-day working, and integrated with other functions and processes such as strategy and finance planning.

The diagram in section 1, figure 1.2, illustrates the portfolio framework. Strategic planning was covered in section 2 and in this section we describe construction and prioritisation, review, reporting and assessing performance of the portfolio.

3.1 Construct and prioritise the portfolio

The aim is to design and build a portfolio that gives the business area managers and sponsors an agreed list of initiatives to manage that will achieve their goals, and also contribute to the organisation's overall goals and strategy.

The process will also include defining the portfolio construction criteria (within the established portfolio framework) and ways of working, so that a consistent approach is adopted across the portfolio.

The 'construct and prioritise the portfolio' process can be further broken down to portfolio entry and prioritisation, and then through delivery and benefits realisation to portfolio exit.

3.1.1 Portfolio entry and exit processes

These are a subset of construction and prioritisation – the entry criteria for an initiative, or potential programme or project, to be included in the portfolio, and the exit point at which benefits stop being tracked. Entry will be through a 'gateway', where certain criteria need to be met, and then the priority is assessed

Portfolio management core processes

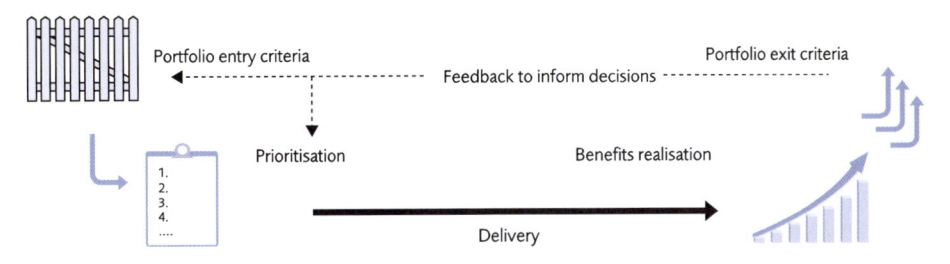

Figure 3.1 Construct and prioritise the portfolio

against the other projects or programmes, including other prospective new entrants, as well as those in flight.

The portfolio entry criteria should include:

- direct contribution to achieving one or more of the strategic goals;
- having a committed sponsor;
- a valid business case with a positive ROI value, depending on the nature and stage of the work and the criteria set by the portfolio manager;
- an assessment of the complexity of the project, or level of risk of not achieving the objectives. High complexity will be associated with high risk, and therefore a lower level of achievability or 'do-ability';
- demand for critical skills – if they are not available or unlikely to be available when required, the timeframe of the potential project may need to be revised;
- resource loading and the impact on the business. A 'heat map' of change impact can be included in the overall balancing and optimisation of the portfolio to assess whether the business can cope with the proposed change.

The criteria need to be unambiguously defined and consistently applied, while recognising that there may be occasional need for flexibility, with exceptions being properly documented and agreed.

Exit from the portfolio would usually be when the benefits have been fully delivered, or after a pre-defined time period for measuring the benefits, e.g. three years after delivery. Again, the criteria need to be consistent but do not need to be identical and may depend on the type of investment, as the benefit realisation profiles of different programmes and projects may differ.

Portfolio Management

3.1.2 Prioritisation

Section 2 talked about the strategy and prioritisation of the goals. The organisation should have a clear investment prioritisation model across:

- BAU (operations);
- existing programmes, projects and other change initiatives, i.e. those already in progress;
- new change initiatives required to meet the corporate goals and strategy;
- other new change initiatives with strong business cases and ROI that will contribute to achieving the strategic goals.

Organisations may choose to define broad levels of investment, e.g. across a number of business units or divisions, but the same prioritisation model should be applied to the 'sub-portfolio' to ensure consistency, while allowing some latitude for the use of local attributes.

The programme and project prioritisation criteria will be based on a range of factors, including:

- ranking/prioritisation/weighting of the corporate goals – some will be more important than others;
- contributions to delivering the strategy and corporate goals – quantitative and qualitative;
- benefits anticipated – to be assessed in comparable formats (for tangible and intangible benefits);
- timing – investment in short-term gains may take priority over longer-term, provided that this does not regularly lower the priority of longer-term projects and programmes (or vice versa);
- legal, regulatory and/or industry standard requirements – such 'compliance' may be mandatory but should be properly assessed;
- level of risk – the probability/likelihood of not delivering a specific benefit. For example, if a cost-to-benefit ratio is 1:4, you may prioritise the activity with a 90 per cent delivery chance higher than one with a 25 per cent delivery chance. However, beware simply giving more weight to a project close to completion compared with those less well formed, which may have greater strategic value;
- innovation – how far the project develops the industry and marketplace.

To ensure that priorities are clear enough to facilitate fact-based decision making, these criteria should normally be agreed and ratified by the board or an executive committee. This ensures that the same criteria are consistently applied and demonstrates that the board and executive stand by the approach. As business units are likely to have more change proposals than either the portfolio or the business can realistically deliver, the prioritisation model helps these to be ranked and considered in the construction of the portfolio.

Ideally the criteria would be set to apply equally to projects and programmes and BAU or operations. However, this may prove challenging, and an alternative approach might be for the board to allocate a percentage of investment to 'change' (i.e. projects and programmes) and a percentage to BAU or operations in each area.

> At a leading financial institution, enterprise architects work with executives each year to define the five-year strategy and develop work packages from which programmes and projects are created. The portfolio is then planned, including rechecking projects in progress against the corporate plan and strategic goals. Once signed off, the portfolio is baselined.
>
> Programmes and projects are mapped against four prioritisation categories. These are (in order of current priority): regulatory; infrastructure; productivity; and growth. Further criteria are then agreed to assess relative priority.
>
> The board is updated quarterly on progress to date and is given a projection for the coming three months. A monthly steering group is in place to monitor the business environment and the portfolio, and identify emerging demand, assessing impacts on the portfolio and priorities.
>
> Portfolio experts need to be mindful of other factors that may override the criteria. These include political will, external forces and the competitive environment.

Additional factors to consider in portfolio construction and prioritisation

Other factors that could be built into the portfolio construction and prioritisation process include:

- only allocating funding to business units for projects/programmes that have had their business case(s) approved – note that this may disadvantage strategic rather than operational improvement projects;
- applying progressive commitment of resources to gradually maturing business cases (especially true of agile programmes and projects). Funding by tranche or stage reviews may also help;
- 'reserving' unallocated funding in a central pot (seed corn) to preserve flexibility and allow for ideas and initiatives later in the cycle to be developed. This supports the concept of a 'rolling portfolio', and allows future years' commitments to be seen going forward in line with the corporate strategy, so that executives can steer the longer-term shape of the portfolio;
- similarly, applying a notional allocation, as a sign of intent, against investment themes at organisational level and/or business unit level which have been aligned to the organisation's goals may help secure initial funding for new ideas;
- rolling the 'active' period of the portfolio forward, thereby reducing the 'cliff-edge' impact of an annual refresh approach, i.e. the portfolio has a fixed horizon period. This might allow demand for funding to be identified earlier, which could trigger changes to the overall strategy (e.g. a research division may highlight that no amount of internal expansion would allow proposed future goals to be met, meaning the strategy has to be changed to include significant outsourcing).

It will be important to have financial systems structured to support the recording of project, programme and portfolio investment allocations and actual and forecast expenditure, covering both in-year budgeting and future years' forecasting.

In most organisations there is an annual cycle, which comes to an end and then restarts for the next period. Changes to the financial systems are likely to be needed to support the 'rolling portfolio' ideas described above.

Portfolio management core processes

> A major organisation prioritised its projects using a matrix with an evaluation of the level of contribution to the strategic goals, the project's benefits within a given period (e.g. three years), and the level of complexity (i.e. risk). This enabled it to compare projects and make rational, consistent decisions.

It is important to have someone, such as a portfolio manager, responsible for overseeing a common application of the portfolio construction and prioritisation approach, identifying inconsistencies and recommending amendments to respond to changing circumstances.

The portfolio is then designed to the agreed criteria, which should ensure that the highest-ranking programmes and projects are included, that there is a clear understanding of the relative priority of others, and that all are balanced with the BAU and operational priorities, in line with their strategic plans.

In most cases this does not happen from scratch – in annual construction or periodic portfolio reviews the portfolio content is refined and priorities changed in the light of emerging data. Often, there is little or no issue with the highest-ranking projects being included – the argument usually comes lower down, where decisions need to be made on just how many projects can realistically be progressed.

As there may be many ways of delivering the strategic goals within the plans and constraints set, the portfolio needs to be balanced in terms of overall risk – see section 2.4. To achieve this, the portfolio construction and prioritisation processes will be iterative, and closely aligned with the strategic planning process.

An analysis of total investment cost, accumulated project or programme value (risk-adjusted benefit) and time (i.e. time-adjusted values until the benefits are realised or the goal is met) is best done with a spreadsheet or possibly a proprietary tool. There are likely to be several different combinations of projects and programmes that can deliver close to optimal solutions, and other factors may need to be considered – the main one being achievability or 'do-ability'.

Outputs from this set of processes would include:

- the prioritisation model to be applied to the portfolio;
- business area (or business unit) goals and targets;
- a defined portfolio, or set of portfolios, reflecting relative priorities;

Portfolio Management

- entry and exit criteria;
- business standards and practices, i.e. ways of working in the portfolio including reporting and forecasting;
- review periods aligned to the organisation's governance 'cadence'.

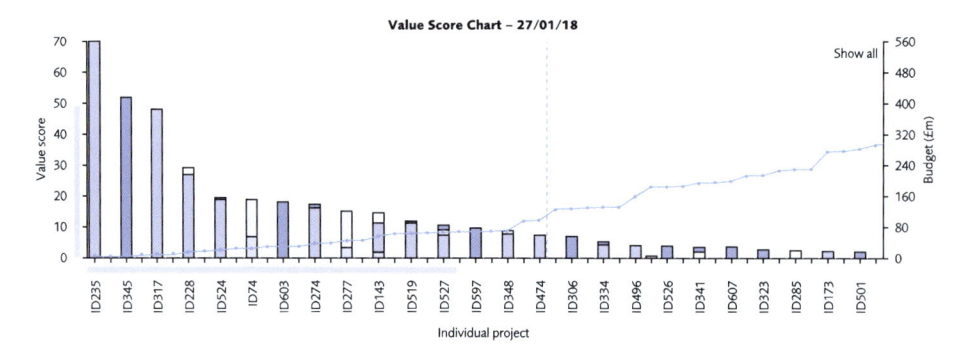

Figure 3.2 A value score chart – benefit and cost comparison

Figure 3.2 shows a value score chart – benefit and cost comparison – normalised so the best project is on the left.

3.2 Develop, monitor and control the portfolio

In figure 1.2 in section 1.4 we reference the process for the portfolio management framework. Once the portfolio has been constructed, including any BAU and other initiatives within the scope of the portfolio, whether it is at an enterprise, business area or functional level, or at all levels, it has to be managed on a regular basis.

The purpose of portfolio monitoring is to make regular checks on how the various initiatives are progressing towards achieving the agreed goals. This activity should be designed to ensure that the portfolio is on track to deliver its benefits and the strategic goals, look for any adjustments to make/recommend as required, and actively mitigate portfolio-level risks.

The portfolio management team or portfolio office will need to examine information ('lead' and 'lag' indicators), either from individual projects and programmes or elsewhere in the organisation. This might be, for example, where initial estimates for cost and benefit are falling beyond materiality limits/ tolerances, or where the business need has changed, so that the project benefit is no longer of sufficient priority to remain within the portfolio.

Portfolio management core processes

This in-flight review process is critical. It requires:

1. An appropriate reporting structure, which is part of overall portfolio governance.
2. Information transfer from projects/programmes to the portfolio office (see section 3.5 on portfolio reporting).
3. A portfolio office adequately resourced with the right capabilities.

Most of the information should already exist in standard project and programme reporting. The requirements of the portfolio function should not add significant extra work or bureaucracy. The portfolio function must create a consolidated view of *key* information, such as the cumulative effect of what is being reported locally, to support portfolio decisions.

Actively mitigating portfolio risk is an important aspect of portfolio monitoring, increasing the chance of the portfolio delivering its goals. Different portfolio functions will use a range of techniques to help mitigate portfolio risk, including those described in the next few sections.

3.2.1 Portfolio dependency mapping

This is a useful tool in the portfolio management team's armoury. It needs to be developed at a high level and include inter-project/programme and other major dependencies, such as factors external to the organisation – e.g. key suppliers

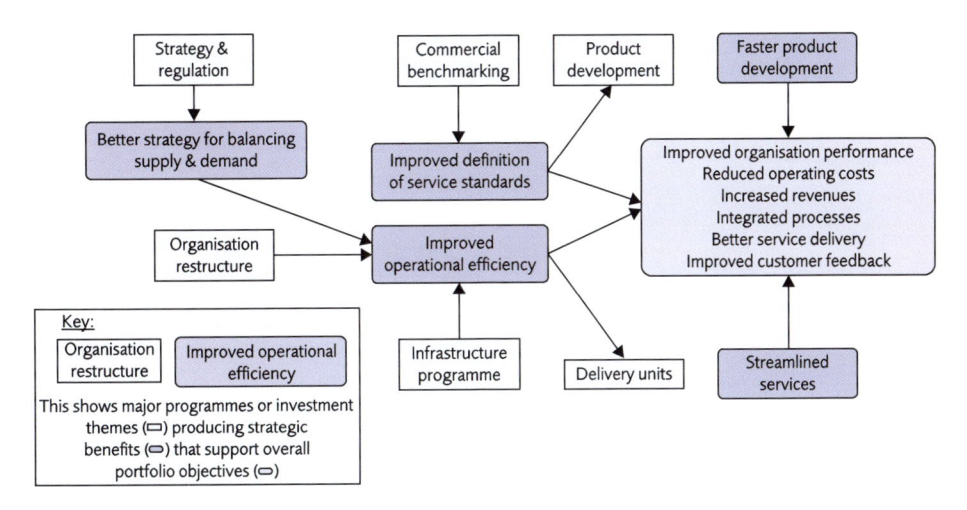

Figure 3.3 Example portfolio dependency map

Portfolio Management

and the political or regulatory environment. As it is reflecting the position at a portfolio level, these dependencies should be significant and relatively few. Its purpose is to provide a roadmap of top-level investments and the crossovers that may suggest potential risks to achieving the organisation's strategic goals.

By managing these dependencies, the portfolio management office can reduce portfolio risks.

3.2.2 Business implementation management

An important function of the portfolio office is to monitor business implementation to ensure no single business area or function is overwhelmed by change, thereby putting benefits realisation at risk. The level and pace of change that an organisation can tolerate without disruption to current projects, or BAU, needs to be assessed, and it is easy to underestimate the time people need to assimilate change. In addition, the level of involvement and participation required by the business subject matter experts in requirements analysis, testing and rollout, the staff time required for training and the product owners and management teams in agile projects, need to be considered.

3.2.3 Portfolio, programme and project management resources

The portfolio office has an important role in understanding the portfolio, programme and project resource needs of the organisation, and should be able to articulate what resource and skills are needed, where and when they are needed, and whether additional external resource should be identified to improve the chances of delivering the portfolio.

3.2.4 Overview of portfolio, programme and project management standards/tools and techniques

The portfolio office may also function as a centre of excellence providing consistent standards, tools, techniques and guidance to the projects and programmes to help them deliver. This can consist of tool and template provision, or involve audits, stage gates and other supporting frameworks.

This helps the portfolio function to understand the 'risk to delivery', and to feed into the portfolio reviews the assessment of the portfolio's likelihood of delivering its benefits and goals, and therefore whether there is any need for in-flight reprioritisation.

3.3 Manage and deliver programmes and projects

Programmes and projects have their own governance, e.g. steering committees and project boards. Portfolio governance does not duplicate, but complements programme and project governance. The portfolio manager would normally be part of the individual programme steering committees and they, or their representative, would be on the board of major projects.

Risks would be managed through the programme or project governance, and only taken to the portfolio board if there was an external or potentially cross-programme risk.

3.3.1 Benefits realisation planning

Benefits realisation planning is part of the individual project or programme scope and owned by the sponsor. The key deliverables will be to contribute to achieving the corporate goals, but benefits would be assessed and the benefits realisation managed by the project or programme. Actual benefits, after the project or programme has delivered the outputs or outcomes, would be monitored by the portfolio and the success or otherwise fed back to the strategic decision process and prioritisation process to inform future decisions.

3.4 Review the portfolio

The purpose of a portfolio review is for the executive committee overseeing the portfolio to consider current status and forecast and to decide whether the portfolio comprises the most effective set of projects and programmes to achieve delivery of the strategic goals in the appropriate timeframe. The business managers in charge of the BAU units should be part of the portfolio review mechanism, giving their input on the achievability of the portfolio and contributing to alternative proposals.

The systems and infrastructure will vary by the size and complexity of the organisation and of the portfolio. A global organisation managing a portfolio across many countries will require different infrastructure solutions from those for a national organisation or one with a relatively simple portfolio or set of portfolios. Size, scale and maturity of the organisation and/or its portfolio will influence the type of portfolio management systems established.

Portfolio Management

The portfolio team will be reviewing elements of the portfolio regularly, perhaps weekly, which will help ensure that preparations for the next formal portfolio review lead to robust recommendations and decisions.

Compiling portfolio reports, as described in section 3.5 below, will include engaging with the main stakeholders to refine proposals to improve understanding, seeking agreement to, and an awareness of, the portfolio management team's recommendations.

The decisions that are taken at the portfolio review determine what reporting is required.

Questions to ask during the portfolio review include:

- Have the strategic goals changed, or are there significant market changes, limits on progress, or changes in the business environment that impact on the strategic goals?
- Are the timelines for achieving the strategic goals on track and likely to stay on track, and if not, what should be done?
- Which projects or programmes are not sufficiently contributing to, or unlikely to contribute to, the strategic goals, or unlikely to deliver the desired ROI?
- Is the organisation getting the best value for money from its investments, i.e. optimising ROI and maximising benefit?
- Should resources be reassigned from one project or programme to another to better achieve the goals, even if the project or programme is on track? Is the current allocation of resources delivering the maximum value and the quickest achievement of the goals?
- Which new projects or programmes should we consider starting, in order to better achieve our goals?
- Are the critical skills in the organisation being utilised in the most efficient and effective way? Typically, around 10 per cent of the skills can usually be identified as critical, and these will, in part, determine the throughput of the portfolio – they will be on the critical path across the portfolio.
- Is the overall risk balanced and in line with the desired risk profile? If not, what is recommended?
- Are portfolio (and organisation) standards being consistently met, and if not, what action will be taken?

The key decisions made at the portfolio review are: which programmes or projects to stop, which to start, and which resources, if any, should be

Portfolio management core processes

reallocated. It is therefore important that the participants at the portfolio review, usually the portfolio executive committee, have the appropriate level of authority.

The output of this process is a portfolio reconstructed or confirmed to meet the strategic goals in the most effective way.

> A blue-chip organisation had a well-defined growth strategy. When a new product was launched by a competitor, the organisation had to re-prioritise its projects and cease some in response to the changes in the marketplace.

3.5 Reporting on the portfolio

Portfolio reporting provides information for portfolio decisions to be taken in the portfolio review, i.e. decisions to stop or start initiatives and/or reallocate resources. It also covers supporting information on change of scope, timelines and priorities. Reporting of individual projects and programmes needs to be aligned with the portfolio reviews as part of the integrated governance arrangements within the organisation.

Portfolio reports should not duplicate programme or project reporting in detail, although some overlap will exist. Such reporting should be mostly 'forward looking', while also providing current status, and be 'sufficient' for decision makers, i.e. it should provide the focussed information that the review executive needs, but no more than that.

The reporting timetable will reflect the frequency of the reviews and should be aligned with and embedded into the organisation's reporting cycle; for example, the portfolio review might be timed to be just before, or part of, a full board meeting.

One of the most important things is the selection of the data required to perform portfolio management effectively. This means working top-down from the decisions that need to be made, and what information is required to make those decisions. It will typically include:

- overall progress and outlook for meeting the corporate goals compared with the strategic plan;

Portfolio Management

- a forecast of which projects or programmes are unlikely to meet their particular objectives as planned, highlighting the potential impact on achieving the strategic goals;
- external and internal portfolio risks, significant project/programme risks, and their potential impact on achieving the goals;
- the projected risk profile versus the planned risk profile;
- forecast versus budget across the overall portfolio, to assess current available funds, supported by programme/project schedules at appropriate levels of detail;
- feedback from the portfolio performance, and benefits tracking, indicating whether the estimates and outlooks have been realistic;
- recommendation by the portfolio manager as to what should be changed (if anything) at the portfolio review, and any recommendations from project/programme leads, with analysis and evidence to support the recommendation.

Standard project and programme reporting should provide most of the information needed to highlight which projects and programmes are likely to miss their objectives. The impact on the corporate goals can be assessed using the information from the strategic planning and portfolio construction stages.

The portfolio management team needs to establish what the portfolio executive requires and why. This determines what gets reported, the standard expected and the format it takes. Usually, this will be focussed on the delivery of strategic goals.

The review executive also needs to be clear about their roles and accountabilities – the desire for lots of information should be resisted (it is time-consuming, expensive, unnecessary and will tend to cloud judgements). The information provided should be just enough to enable reviewers to make the required decisions.

Essentially, the portfolio management team is providing:

- information to help executives understand what is happening, what is likely to happen, when, and the consequences ahead, together with recommendations;
- assurance that the portfolio is on track, and likely to remain on track, and being managed successfully – or if not, options and recommendations on what needs to be done;
- recommended intervention, where discussions and/or decisions are required for future direction and to safeguard the strategic goals. This includes starting or stopping projects and programmes and redirecting resources;
- any major proposals from project/programme management, with associated commentary and context.

Portfolio management core processes

Supporting analysis might include resource deployment, where executive intervention is required to ensure priorities are supported.

It is essential to adopt the portfolio management principles and then develop or utilise the management infrastructure and systems to support the projects and programmes and the information required to make portfolio decisions.

Some of the following points may help in thinking about what is best for your organisation.

- The information provided should give the portfolio management team the ability to quickly assess the impact of real or potential changes, and to recommend appropriate action to the portfolio exec and investment board.
- Information needs to be 'one truth', i.e. the team should avoid having potentially contradictory or ambiguous data from different systems or sources.
- The information should enable the team to look forward and forecast – portfolio decisions are made on 'lead' metrics, not 'lag' metrics.
- Interfaces with other systems, such as project/finance/resources, need to be clear and straightforward; this will reinforce the credibility of the information and ensure there is one version of the truth.
- Time-consuming data entry needs to be avoided. Portfolio management requires very little additional information.
- Visualisation of the portfolio metrics may be helpful, e.g. 'bubble diagrams', when considering factors such as contribution to the strategy and risk profile.

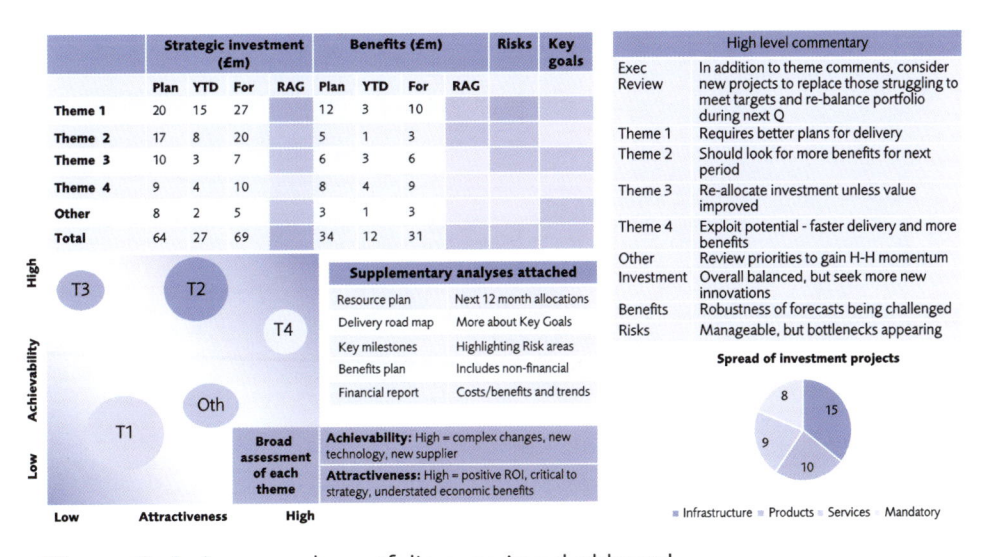

Figure 3.4 An example portfolio overview dashboard

Portfolio Management

The aim is to keep the final report straightforward, using graphics and presentation styles that facilitate effective decision making. Considerable effort may be required by the portfolio manager and team in analysing the information and making recommendations.

The output of this process is focussed, relevant information in an agreed reporting format, which enables a portfolio executive to review the portfolio status and outlook, and make decisions to optimise the portfolio.

3.6 Assessing the performance of the portfolio

The purpose of this process is to feed back information and increase learning to help improve the portfolio management process and decision making.

Results from the performance assessment should help improve the overall portfolio management process, including its relationship with strategic planning, portfolio construction, prioritisation processes and reporting.

To help improve future portfolio decision making, for example, it could look at whether benefits are systematically over- or underestimated, or if timelines are consistently misjudged. This may lead to changes in the way that estimates are produced, or action to improve forecasting.

3.6.1 Customer satisfaction

This would be based on feedback from the 'customers' of the portfolio management process – the portfolio governance body, business unit managers and functional leaders. For example, they might be asked if they are more confident that:

- they have control over the organisation's destiny;
- they will achieve their strategic goals;
- money is being well spent and not wasted;
- individual investments will deliver on their promises;
- business cases are believable;
- resources are being well utilised.

3.6.2 Governance compliance

If this is weak, it may be a signal that the processes are too onerous or not being managed effectively.

For example, it might manifest as some business units attempting to circumvent the process to get ahead of competing projects. Such behaviour would need to be quashed – consistent treatment of all initiatives and all stakeholders is essential.

Measurement of actual benefits realised against those planned may also indicate that the governance is not as effective as it might be.

3.6.3 Consistency and effectiveness of the processes

Part of the portfolio management remit could include ensuring consistent, yet appropriate, processes are applied across programmes and projects. If there is real or circumstantial evidence to suggest the processes are not being followed adequately, it suggests the processes may need to be modified and improved.

Typically, project and programme managers seek the most efficient way of doing things, and this needs to be understood when designing the organisation's processes and procedures.

3.6.4 Portfolio 'churn'

Consideration of this could include, for example:

- identifying how many projects were considered but failed to have their business case approved;
- looking at how many were approved but had to be stopped before implementation, other than as directed by the portfolio reviews, plus the extent of delays to plans.

A high level of portfolio churn may suggest inadequate initial planning, and proposals not being assessed with sufficient rigour, and this should be relayed back to the programme and project sponsors to address. Conversely, it might reflect that there have been fast changes in the environment that are leading to 'redundant' projects being removed quickly – which is an indicator of good portfolio management.

3.6.5 Strategy variation

If the organisation's strategic goals have changed, particularly if it is more often than would be expected, to what degree is this due to internal or external factors?

Portfolio Management

Too regular changes can destabilise the portfolio and the agreed portfolio processes. They also create unnecessary work and have a negative impact on staff.

3.6.6 Stakeholder relationships

Difficult or ineffective relationships between the portfolio management team and business units may be highlighted in both day-to-day interactions and board or executive meetings. They may be manifested as poor compliance, complaints about process, out-of-date data, and meetings being hard to arrange.

The portfolio management team may need to use qualitative information, experience and observation to highlight practices and behaviour that business areas/project teams may not recognise or may wish to keep hidden – such tension needs to be managed in the context of a collective desire to meet corporate objectives.

3.6.7 Portfolio delivery

While the prime responsibilities for creating the benefits from the individual change initiatives rests with project and programme sponsors, the portfolio team has a key role in keeping everything on track and optimising the whole portfolio.

Evidence might emerge of possibly fundamental flaws in the overall portfolio management process, leading to poor decisions and sub-optimal portfolio delivery.

3.6.8 Summary of other factors

A range of factors should be assessed to help ensure the portfolio team/process is fully effective, including:

- stakeholder perceptions, both at project level and among the executive team;
- time taken to get proposals accepted into the portfolio, and major causes of delays;
- the degree to which the portfolio remains strategically aligned;
- overall quality of information being acquired and presented;
- proportion of recommendations by the portfolio team being accepted at executive portfolio reviews;
- quality of the recommendations and thoroughness of preparation.

Portfolio management core processes

The generalised process maturity model illustrates the levels:

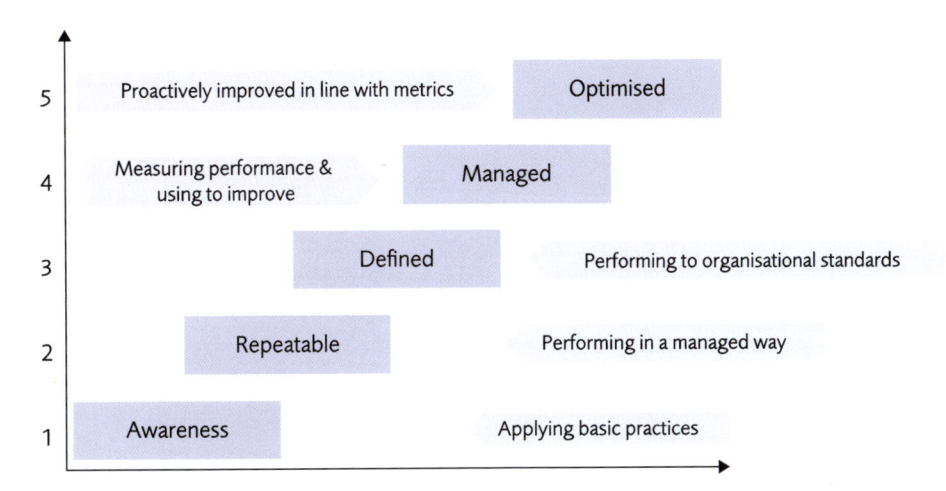

Figure 3.5 Portfolio performance assessment maturity model

Different models are available to assess the maturity of portfolio management, e.g. Axelos' P3M3. This is suggested as one indicator that can be utilised to measure the effectiveness of the portfolio. However, the real measure is the results, and whether the corporate goals are being achieved.

Outputs from the portfolio process performance review would include:

- process improvement recommendations;
- an implementation plan for agreed recommendations;
- an assessment of the relative success of the portfolio over time, in terms of achieving the strategic goals and the anticipated ROI.

4

Implementing portfolio management

This section will cover the drivers and main steps to building, developing and sustaining a portfolio management capability within an organisation.

Portfolio management includes defining portfolio governance, clear roles, responsibilities, accountabilities and reporting structures that support decision making. Introducing it will have a significant impact on the organisation and will fundamentally alter how change is managed. It is therefore likely to require a change in the organisation's behaviours and culture.

Portfolio management has many aspects, and an organisation will need to clearly and unambiguously identify what will deliver value for them, and adapt the practice of portfolio management to their individual needs. This will require careful management, coordination and capable resources. Portfolio management is most effective when driven by business goals and strategy, either at an organisation or business area level, although it has often been introduced via the IT function.

One of the hardest things about introducing portfolio management to an organisation or system is the mirror that is held up to the executives, and dealing with the behaviours of people as a result. Organisations that have shared their experiences have found that treating the introduction of portfolio management as a project and adopting a change management approach helped them achieve a successful outcome.

4.1 Business drivers for portfolio management – understanding the business imperative

There are many reasons why an organisation might decide that portfolio management is required. Often it will be introduced in response to issues resulting from the actual or perceived failure of current processes, or it might

Implementing portfolio management

even be brought in during a crisis, where the business needs to make a radical reappraisal of its change initiatives and performance.

There are several structured change and project methodologies that can be used and, as with any project, change management needs to be integrated into the approach.

4.1.1 Getting portfolio management started

The drivers for change will manifest themselves in many ways, such as:

- a desire to implement a major transformational change across the organisation;
- a corporate review of strategy implementation, highlighting significantly disconnected change management and mismatch between expectations and reality;
- a senior executive discovering from their peers that alternative, more effective, ways of achieving the corporate goals and managing their portfolio should be explored;
- awareness by new management that there are better ways of achieving the strategy, and managing delivery and benefits through portfolio management;
- an enforced reassessment of the investment priorities, for example due to a takeover or a major change in the market or environment;
- the existing planning, strategy or portfolio team being unable to satisfy executive questions about the effectiveness of the organisation's investment, where it is being spent, what benefits are being achieved and what the ROI is. Several organisations have reported being surprised at the findings once they carry out an inventory of in-flight projects.

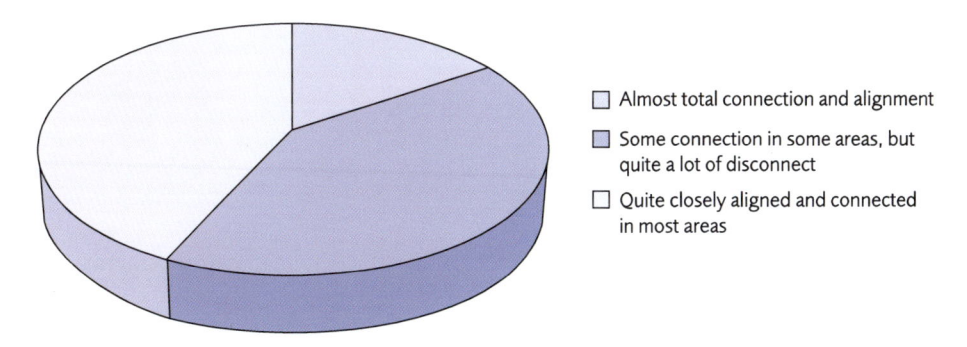

Figure 4.1 Strategy and portfolio alignment

Portfolio Management

A review of a number of organisations found very few have complete connection between their strategy and portfolio. The vast majority were able to identify a level of disconnect. As a consequence of this, the aims of the portfolio may not deliver the aims of the business. The signs that an organisation would benefit from portfolio management in section 1 table 1.1, together with the benefits in section 1 figure 1.1, are useful indicators and characteristics to reference when building the case for change and its adoption.

4.2 Introducing portfolio management

Organisations starting to formalise portfolio management must start with active sponsorship from senior manager(s). The context that portfolio management is starting from within an organisation is important – as is its target and why it wants to get there. The starting point can span a spectrum of portfolio management maturity (figure 3.5, p. 39) and may be evolving, so that some business units or functions may be further developed than others. This 'mix' of portfolio management maturity must be recognised, and advantages or constraints managed.

There are several ways that an organisation can then start the change process. The right balance needs to be struck for the organisation and the differing levels of maturity, to achieve the right blend of top-down, in-house and external/consultant-driven approaches to change, such that the commitment, credibility, skills and experience are in place.

> A regulatory body wanted to introduce portfolio management to improve the way it managed its projects and programmes. Initially a small core team was set up and they worked with a few major programmes. As they demonstrated the value they brought to the organisation, additional projects and programmes were included. Over a period of around 18 months to two years, the team expanded slightly and portfolio management became the organisation's way of managing change.

An in-house steering team built from influential advocates from across the organisation's breadth and hierarchical levels has many advantages and can provide the leadership and credibility to engage the organisation. Implementing portfolio management is likely to bring about changes to how senior executives

Implementing portfolio management

make board-level decisions, and will have an impact on organisational-level governance processes. It is critical, therefore, that the person leading the development of portfolio management has the necessary skills and experience. Appointing a portfolio sponsor is an increasingly common way of helping drive forward such organisational change.

The group must also have the right blend of change skills and portfolio management practical experience. This may be met from the in-house team within the organisation, but consideration should also be given to drawing on other specialist skills and professional bodies. Consultants or specialists with proven experience and practical application of portfolio and change management, supported through effective utilisation of appropriate processes, tools, techniques and metrics, may also be helpful.

Key is that the board and CEO actively support and lead the drive to implement portfolio management. This will set the direction and vision for portfolio management and the desired outcomes and benefits for the organisation.

> A global FMCG company introduced portfolio management within their IT function as a driver to reduce the percentage of total revenue spent on IT. This change meant each country could no longer choose which investments they would make, but instead each initiative was prioritised at the regional level, and decisions on where to allocate funds were based on the organisation's strategic priorities. Within three years, the organisation achieved its goal of reducing IT spend from four per cent to two per cent of global revenue, while delivering a higher ROI by leveraging their scale.

4.2.1 Sponsorship and management of stakeholders

Treating the introduction of portfolio management as a project in itself has frequently proved to be a successful strategy. Key components for setting up such a project include:

- clear, active sponsorship from a senior executive;
- active support from the executive board (as sponsors of the enterprise portfolio);
- appropriate day-to-day leadership from someone who has the right influencing skills, is respected by the executive, management team and key staff, and has

Portfolio Management

the necessary capabilities. They would be likely to be appointed the initial portfolio manager who would build the team to deliver portfolio management;
- providing unambiguous terms of reference for the key stakeholders and ensuring the board are aware of, and accept, their responsibilities as portfolio sponsors, and for setting/supporting the appropriate environment;
- a realistic set of outcomes and metrics in terms of measuring achievement of strategic objectives, benefits, ROI, and effective decision making.

> Key staff in a large commercial organisation saw the need for portfolio management but couldn't persuade the executives. They changed their message from 'portfolio management' – which was seen by some as 'just the latest fad' – and talked in terms of 'enabling you to achieve your goals and targets more effectively'. This caught the executives' attention, as it was expressed in terms that were important to them and that they could relate to. It was also potentially helping the executives achieve their own targets (and bonuses) by aligning organisation and individual goals.

4.2.2 Meeting the needs of stakeholders

The many influences and dynamics associated with introducing portfolio management can be challenging, with both hard processes and soft skills needed to engage stakeholders. It is not something that can be wholly delivered by simply following processes. Nor can it be done by the portfolio management team alone.

Wherever portfolio management touches the organisation, there will be an impact on workplace demands that has to be considered.

Achieving the best outcome for the organisation, teams and individuals will require collaboration and engagement. Creating the necessary reliable and strong partnerships that are aligned to clear and unambiguous goals is essential to success. The whole portfolio is greater than the sum of its individual projects and programmes.

Implementing portfolio management will bring about changes to how senior executives make board-level decisions and will have an impact on organisational-level governance processes. It is critical, therefore, that the person leading the development of portfolio management has the necessary skills and experience to engage at this level.

Implementing portfolio management

Considerable effort is likely to be required, especially in the early stages, to ensure that stakeholders know how they are expected to support the process and that in doing so they, in turn, will gain some value. This often needs repeating.

Implementing portfolio management requires collaboration, and for the objectives of the organisation to be prioritised over any individual stakeholder's personal or departmental needs. Creating a stakeholder map and identifying how best to manage and communicate with them will help. The level of effort involved, especially in the early stages, should not be underestimated, but it will be worth the effort in gaining collaboration, buy-in and feedback as you develop and implement portfolio management.

Portfolio management operates at all levels, but the strategic level is particularly crucial. In fact, without that level of stakeholder support, introducing portfolio management will be a challenge to say the least.

Engagement principles that have proved helpful when establishing portfolio management include:

- setting realistic expectations;
- active, effective sponsorship;
- using language that fits the organisation, avoiding portfolio management jargon;
- making it work for your organisation, recognising different starting points in different business units and, once implementation has started, letting it evolve, but avoiding compromising the principles of portfolio management;
- developing and facilitating understanding of 'what's in it for me?' for all levels; many at project level may see this as simply providing management information from which they get no value or even feel threatened by;
- engaging and involving influential senior executives and managers in concept and design, so that they can help support or sponsor the development of portfolio management;
- focussing on the information to make the business portfolio decisions – and not being tempted to produce too much information in reports or dashboards. The key decisions to be made are to start, stop or reallocate resources across initiatives based on the current and forecast priorities;
- ensuring that all stakeholders understand why portfolio management is being introduced and why it is critical to future business success. This entails showing the overall position of the organisation, the challenges and what is driving the need for change, and ensuring the whole workforce is aware of

Portfolio Management

what the corporate strategy is and how they individually contribute to achieving those goals.

4.3 Establishing portfolio management

4.3.1 Establishing the portfolio governance

To be most effective, portfolio governance should be aligned to the organisation's existing governance structure, internal and external reporting needs and financial management practices.

In establishing the appropriate level of governance, the portfolio team should lead and facilitate the information requirements with the board and senior leadership team, focussing on providing just enough information to make the required decisions.

The project team implementing portfolio management will have facilitated building the shared vision, processes, roles and behaviours. The organisation will then need to embed this into BAU. The appropriate structure, behaviours and metrics need to be built into the organisation, such that continual improvement is achieved.

4.3.2 Working with the Organisation

Fundamentally, much of what portfolio management embodies is about 'how we change the organisation to run the business more effectively and achieve the strategic goals'.

Even an organisation that is mature in portfolio management can be challenged through differing priorities, influences and behaviours. Organisational politics needs to be acknowledged; portfolio management will hold up a mirror and not all executives will like what they see.

The portfolio manager's understanding of the various perspectives and viewpoints is therefore vital. Some organisations adopting transformational change and establishing portfolio management put in place an executive-level sponsor to support the portfolio manager with engagement at the executive level and to have overall accountability for the success of the portfolio.

There are many influences and dynamics that can affect and challenge the management of the portfolio. These include:

- working with others to achieve strategically aligned functional as well as corporate goals;
- unplanned demand for resources, over which some control may have been ceded to a central function or decision-making body.

4.3.3 Clear strategic goals drive the portfolio

Having clear and supported business goals is fundamental to ensuring that an organisation's portfolio is properly designed. Failure to establish these may lead to conflict over the priorities of the projects in the portfolio.

A challenge for the portfolio manager is to present the portfolio in such a way that the strategic goals and strategy, and therefore project, programme and BAU alignment, is clear and free from contentious issues.

Any ambiguities or uncertainties need to be identified for the attention of the senior executive, who should provide clarity and direction.

4.3.4 Structure and roles

Many organisations manage at an enterprise-wide portfolio level, but they may also have a series of sub-organisational-level portfolios, for example specific business, operational or functional unit portfolios.

Often a partial form of portfolio management may be in place, even if it is not called that, as in the following examples.

- The organisation is delivering multiple changes through small changes or enhancements, BAU or projects, that have been grouped into a business unit portfolio.
- The organisation is managing within a constrained set of resources (whether people, systems or cost) to support the projects and programmes through which the changes are delivered. Not all the projects can be delivered at the same time, so decisions are required as to what happens when, based on the organisation's priorities, leading to plans that require monitoring and adjustment, using a portfolio management approach.
- There is an annual cycle during which the year's change budgets are set, and the projects and change initiatives that the organisation wishes to proceed with are prioritised and agreed.

Portfolio Management

> A major utility organisation outsourced its IT projects and support to a partnering organisation but was dissatisfied with elements of their performance. The IT portfolio was subsequently split into 'mini-portfolios' aligned with the business areas. The governance was then set up with an IT portfolio manager for each business area served, together with a senior business director. They prioritised the projects by business area, taking into account capability, cost, benefits and risk, and ran regular portfolio reviews to reassign resources and reprioritise initiatives in line with evolving business needs and the business goals. This proved very successful and significantly increased the business satisfaction with IT and business performance.

If the organisation is doing some of these things already, introducing or enhancing formal portfolio management processes and principles will help strengthen the organisation's overall management of change.

Depending on the scale of change, portfolio management may need to establish processes and routines to assess the impact of other planned or in-flight programmes or changes across the organisation and take these into consideration.

4.4 Governance roles and relationship to organisational governance

The board sets the vision, goals, corporate strategy, ethics and culture (i.e. portfolio management) for the organisation and sits at the head of the governance. It is important that the vision and goals are set for the organisation – in large organisations this might be done at corporate level, divisional level, business unit, site level – but the key is that the goals are all fully aligned. The portfolio executive is a sub-committee of the board (with delegated governance accountability for ensuring benefits realisation) and helps determine how to deliver the agreed strategic objectives, often working with the board, supported by the portfolio manager and portfolio management office. They ensure the integrity of portfolio management governance and processes. The portfolio manager is accountable for delivery of the overall agreed portfolio.

Implementing portfolio management

The portfolio entry criteria and governance mechanism are usually developed by the portfolio manager and agreed with the portfolio executive or the board.

The portfolio manager oversees the delivery of the portfolio, supports the project sponsors in realising the benefits and maintains focus on achieving the outcomes and goals. In addition, they track and monitor the risk profile.

Projects and programmes have their own governance via their project or programme sponsor to the board – portfolio management works alongside this (and assures it is in place) but does not duplicate it.

The portfolio management office (PMO) supports the portfolio and business management team, and also the programme and project teams, although they may have their own PMO. The portfolio management office needs to be fully integrated with any existing programme or project PMOs. Many successful organisations have a fully integrated PMO function supporting both the portfolio, and the programmes and projects.

The key role of the PMO is to evaluate progress and assess the outlook of the overall portfolio towards delivery of the business strategy, and to recommend actions to realign and optimise where required. Further detail on how to do this is given in section 3.2.

The structure will vary by organisation depending on their ways of working. Typically, organisations adopt either a centralised or a decentralised approach.

4.4.1 Centralised approach

Programme and project managers and PMO staff report to a central portfolio management function and are then allocated to individual programmes and projects, with a dotted line reporting to the business sponsors or programme steering groups. This helps ensure consistency, but also depends on the staff developing good relationships with the sponsors and business teams.

Portfolio Management

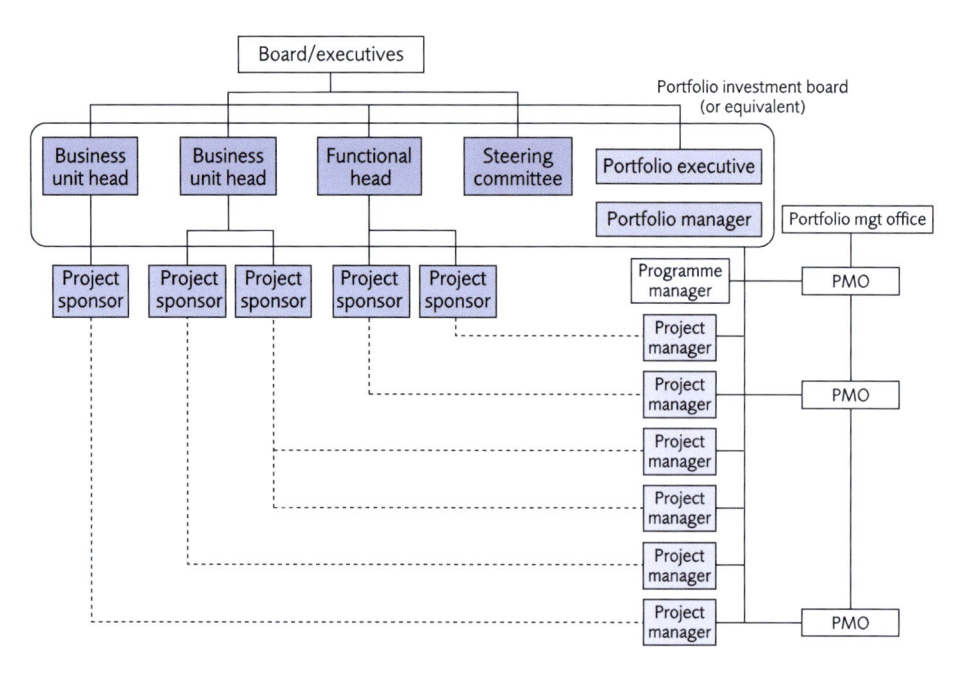

Figure 4.2 Centralised portfolio management

4.4.2 Decentralised approach

The programme and project managers and PMO staff report to the business, but have a dotted line reporting to the portfolio manager. This helps ensure the business drives the programmes and projects but it is more difficult for the portfolio manager to influence and there is a greater risk of 'pet projects' being sponsored by the business. The portfolio executive often has a stronger role to play in ensuring consistency and fairness across the different business unit (BU) and functional heads.

Organisations will develop their portfolio management capabilities at different rates, and these will be reflected in their overall portfolio management maturity.

Implementing portfolio management

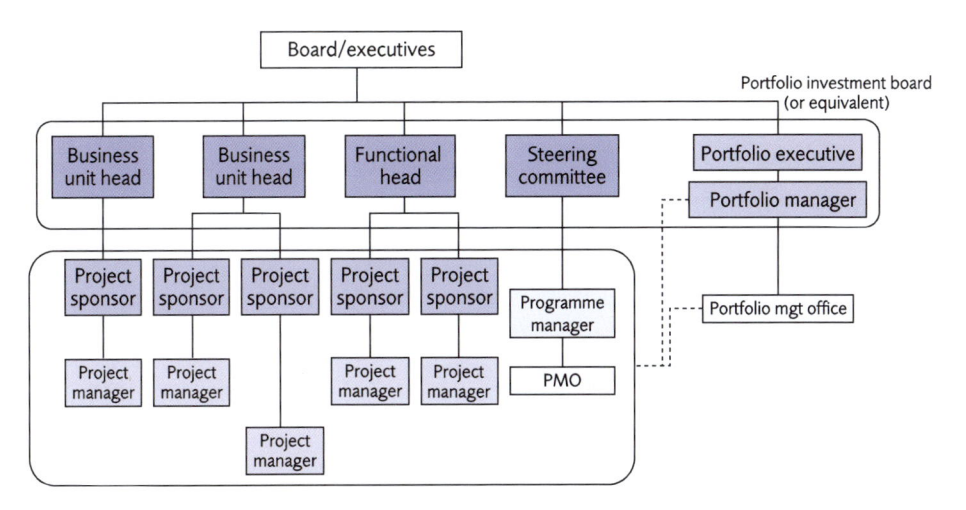

Figure 4.3 Decentralised portfolio management

The skills, knowledge, experience and behaviours that are required to implement portfolio management will vary by organisation. However, key attributes of the portfolio manager and portfolio management team include:

- strong influencing skills, particularly with executives and senior stakeholders, but also with project sponsors, the project community, business managers and delivery teams;
- good communication skills and ability to summarise complicated data into simple information;
- ability to challenge senior staff and board members and be resilient and even-handed in applying the prioritisation criteria;
- an in-depth understanding of the organisation's strategic goals and planning processes;
- ability to see the 'big picture' and work towards it to achieve the corporate strategy;
- familiarity with project and programme management techniques and approaches;
- financial and business case expertise;
- benefits realisation and monitoring skills;
- prioritisation and excellent facilitation skills;
- clarity on portfolio principles and aims.

Portfolio Management

Table 4.1 summarises the main roles and the associated RACI for creating an effective portfolio management environment.

Activity	Responsible	Accountable	Consult	Inform
Set the vision and strategic goals	Board/executives		Senior management	Management and staff
Develop the strategic objectives and plans	Portfolio executive/manager	Board/executives	Senior and BU managers and sponsors	Senior and BU management, sponsors, programme, project and PMO community
Implement portfolio, programme and project governance	Portfolio executive/manager	Board/executives	Senior and BU management, sponsors, programme, project and PMO community	Management community
Benefits management	Programme and project managers	Sponsors	Portfolio manager, portfolio review board	Board, PMO
Construct portfolio	Portfolio manager, portfolio review board	Portfolio executive	BU managers and sponsors, programme and project managers	Board, PMO
Review portfolio	Portfolio manager, portfolio review board	Portfolio executive	BU managers/sponsors, programme and project managers, PMO	Programme and project managers, PMO
Monitor and report	Programme and project managers, PMO, portfolio manager	Sponsors and portfolio manager	BU managers/sponsors	Portfolio review board
Deliver projects	Programme and project teams	Programme and project managers	BU managers/sponsors	Portfolio manager

Table 4.1 RACI matrix for creating an effective portfolio environment

4.5 How to measure early success

Initially the results of implementing portfolio management will be difficult to quantify. Early success is partly the perception of better management control over the shape, size and direction of the portfolio.

The key metric is delivery of the strategic goals and desired outcomes, and achievement of the defined corporate strategy.

Additional success measures might be:

- improved clarity on project priorities;
- metrics informing and influencing organisational capability and capacity:
    - more realistic estimates;
    - increased likelihood of delivery on time;
    - improved realisation of the projected benefits;
- improved provision of data for key decisions and improved capability;
- projects and programmes stopped because they no longer align to strategic goals:
    - improved utilisation of resources to be reassigned, through realignment, to better achieve the goals and increase return on investment;
- improved measurements of actual benefits and business performance;
- staff less stressed, as the priorities are clear and specialist staff are used appropriately.

4.6 Challenges for portfolio management

This section outlines nine key challenges that organisations have encountered in implementing or adopting portfolio management practices. These challenges cover areas dealt with in the guide, but also highlight the cultural challenge and the softer skills needed for successful portfolio management.

4.6.1 Lack of clarity of the organisation's vision, goals and strategy

The board is responsible for setting the vision, goals and strategy and communicating them to the management team. However, the vision may not be completely clear and consistent and, over time, priorities, strategy and goals are likely to change. The portfolio team, through the executive, needs to ensure that the goals are clear and prioritised, and address and resolve any ambiguities with the board.

4.6.2 Lack of board-level consensus

Sometimes there will be an explicit or implicit lack of agreement on which direction an organisation should take, and what the corporate strategy and goals should be, or their prioritisation. The portfolio team should be prepared to model different scenarios for senior management to consider, and to recommend a solution. Any lack of consensus is likely to impact on achievement of the goals. This is, of course, even more difficult if there are competing agendas at board level – this will require CEO involvement and direction.

4.6.3 Priorities not clearly defined or understood

The prioritisation framework must be reviewed regularly and kept in line with organisational strategy and goals. Over time, there is a risk that local priorities take precedence over organisational priorities and that conflicts emerge as a result. Any such ambiguities need to be resolved quickly through persuasion or escalation.

4.6.4 Resources and their allocation not optimised

It is important to keep project and programme resources properly aligned with priorities, and focussed on the projects or programmes that contribute to the goals and provide the best ROI and benefits. These are likely to be switched or reassigned as the portfolio develops and progresses, to ensure the goals are achieved.

There will be a number of critical resources in the organisation on which various projects depend. These might be of the order of 10 per cent of the total resource pool, but may well determine the throughput of the portfolio, as they will be on the critical path. Focussing on the maximum utilisation of these critical resources will help optimise the portfolio and so deliver the goals, ROI and benefits in the most effective way.

Keeping a record of resource demand, supply and dependency management at the portfolio level will enable scheduling decisions based on agreed priorities.

4.6.5 Lack of portfolio management skills

As portfolio management is still a maturing discipline, many organisations do not yet have what they believe is the right level of necessary skills. Over time, the increasing professionalism of project management, and sharing of best practice among portfolio managers, should help to address this. Figure 4.4 shows there is a perception of a significant shortage of adequate portfolio management skills within industry today.

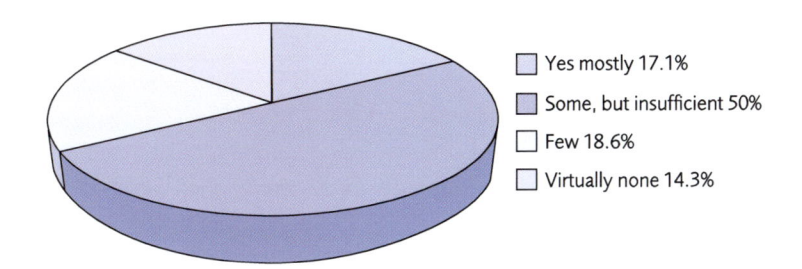

- Yes mostly 17.1%
- Some, but insufficient 50%
- Few 18.6%
- Virtually none 14.3%

Figure 4.4 Organisational skills levels

4.6.6 Inadequate or overly bureaucratic portfolio controls

Progression of projects and programmes should follow agreed processes, including business case approval, stage gate exit and next stage entry and associated plans. This is part of project and programme governance.

Portfolio governance and controls should not duplicate existing governance; they must be complementary to the information and processes already established within the programme or project and the organisation. They must, however, give enough information to meet the needs of the executive and sponsors of the portfolio.

Decisions will need to be made as to whether to accept new initiatives into the portfolio, or to stop or defer existing initiatives, and any such decisions need to be communicated quickly to the programme or project. The information on which such decisions can be based must therefore be available as part of the portfolio data and reporting, and provided for the portfolio meeting. Portfolio decisions need to be captured and recorded, to ensure their costs and benefits can be tracked by the portfolio.

4.6.7 The cultural challenge

Even with the best of collaborative regimes in place, natural behaviours can be a challenge to the sustainability of portfolio management.

Collaboration and understanding of the various perspectives and viewpoints is therefore vital, and in part depends on the skills of the portfolio manager.

Many factors will influence how portfolio management performs. These include:

- the need to work with others to achieve strategically-aligned local, as well as corporate, goals;
- unplanned demand for resources, over which some control may have been ceded to a central function or decision-making body;
- the counter argument that 'it's not how we do things around here';
- clashing priorities that mean that one party must give way – this can be psychologically difficult to face.

Portfolio management needs to be seen to be adding value, and as an integral part of the day-to-day process and governance cycles.

4.6.8 Limited perception of portfolio management

The risk that portfolio management can be seen as 'just a group of project people sitting in isolation to produce a plan once a year' can be a major challenge for an organisation striving to embed formal portfolio management practices into its ways of working. The intention of this guide is to disprove notions such as these. However, without careful communication of what is expected of stakeholders and why, the portfolio management process can be seen as bureaucratic and something 'done to me', rather than a positive, participative process that benefits the organisation.

It is critical that portfolio management integrates seamlessly within the organisational governance and decision-making processes, supports strategic planning and has the aim of achieving corporate goals.

4.6.9 Portfolio management is seen as just the latest management idea

This is another common challenge for portfolio management, and again, communication is key. As shown in the mini-case study in section 4.2.1, presenting portfolio management as a way of helping the executives and senior management achieve their corporate goals (and therefore bonuses) can help with the introduction. Showing evidence-based benefits of the approach, such as improved alignment or increased predictability, is also a strong driver to gain senior-level commitment and enthusiasm.

These nine challenges can be used to learn and build appropriate strategies for your organisation to use in change management.

Ultimately the organisation needs to see the benefits of portfolio management for the business; it needs to own and sponsor the journey and embed it in its behaviours, processes, roles and culture.

5
Recommended focus areas

There are a number of key threads, highlighted below, that are critical to ensuring the success of portfolio management within an organisation.

- Ensure the board and senior executives are effectively sponsoring the content of the portfolio and actively championing portfolio management itself. If they do not, decisions made away from the board will not be effective.
- Work towards establishing an honest, collaborative approach, through which trust within the executive and staff across the organisation can be built. Do not underestimate the cultural impact and change management effort needed.
- Focus on the strategic goals:
    - If there are no goals, or if they are unclear, deal with this issue first.
    - They should be unambiguous, 'smart' and properly communicated throughout the organisation by the executive team; if they are not, the focus on what is important will be lost.
- Prioritise strategic goals clearly, and build into unambiguous portfolio rules:
    - These should be the basis for decisions affecting the portfolio.
    - If most or all goals are assessed as 'high priority', decisions will tend be taken arbitrarily within the organisation or from the perception of local management. Ideally, there needs to be a reasonable balance between 'high', 'medium' and 'low', or equivalent.
    - At times, be prepared to give precedence to critical activity on 'low' priority projects over less important activity on higher priority projects.
- Align 'tactical' projects to strategic goals. If that is impossible, why do them?
    - If the majority of initiatives are 'tactical', review their strategic alignment carefully and confirm they are the most effective use of resources. Can they/should they be grouped?

Recommended focus areas

- Fully embed portfolio governance into the organisation's governance – make it robust:
  - Portfolio management ensures the organisation is 'doing the right things'.
  - Projects and programmes have their own governance to 'do things right'.
  - Manage the level of information sought, do not add an additional governance layer.
  - Keep a light touch, but apply principles rigorously and consistently.
- Critically assess what information is really needed to make portfolio decisions:
  - Usually, a mix of 'performance to date' and 'future forecasts' is appropriate;
  - The former needs to help executives understand and evaluate latest context/trends.
  - The latter should be designed to focus on the key decisions going forward.
  - In both cases, seek to provide 'just enough' information to facilitate decision making.
- Demonstrate the value of portfolio management by, for example, showing improvements in strategic alignment and overall ROI, using a range of well-chosen metrics.
- Be, and be seen to be, consistent and fair across the portfolio, irrespective of an individual programme or project sponsor's influence. Any perception of 'favouritism' will undermine the whole approach and reduce its effectiveness and rigour.
- All new and in-flight projects and programmes should be considered consistently, alongside BAU where appropriate, to ensure full alignment across the organisation to its strategic goals.
- Managing project managers whose projects are being stopped needs careful handling – the decision is not to do with them as people and their skills, but the situation that the organisation/system is facing.

Appendix

Summary roles and responsibilities

Table A1 The roles involved in portfolio management, how they contribute and the value they deliver

Roles	Contribution to portfolio management	Value received or delivered
Board of directors	<ul><li>Portfolio sponsor</li><li>Sets and communicates the strategic goals for the organisation</li><li>Prioritises the corporate mission and strategic goals</li><li>Sets the proportion of the total investment/funding that is for 'change' and for 'operations or business as usual'</li><li>Allocates investment/funding to the portfolio/s</li><li>Sets the risk profile, or risk profile limits, for the overall portfolio.</li></ul>	<ul><li>Achievement of the organisation's goals</li><li>Increased ROI and benefit</li><li>More effective and efficient achievement of the strategic goals</li><li>Greater visibility of the benefits expected from change investment</li><li>Improved confidence that the investment is optimised to achieve its strategic goals.</li></ul>

Summary roles and responsibilities

Roles	Contribution to portfolio management	Value received or delivered
Portfolio investment board (where required – a subset of the board of directors plus the portfolio manager)	■ Regularly reviews and adjusts the portfolio to ensure a focus on goals ■ Decides which projects and/or programmes should be stopped, which should be started, and reallocates investment resources where needed to achieve the organisational strategy and optimise the ROI and other desired benefits.	■ Alignment of programme and project objectives to strategic goals ■ Optimum ROI and benefit.
Portfolio executive (board member and investment board chair)	■ Ensures effective governance and effectiveness of portfolio decisions ■ Implements the strategic priorities ■ Accountable for the performance of the portfolio, the ROI and overall risk profile for the portfolio ■ Champions the portfolio processes.	
Portfolio manager	■ Implements portfolio governance processes and delegated accountabilities ■ Ensures consistency across the portfolio ■ Recommends projects and programmes that should be stopped, started or have resources reallocated ■ Implements the stop, start, reallocate and other decisions from the executives ■ Manages risk and dependencies within the portfolio ■ Manages resource requirements, allocation and issues.	■ Optimised portfolio ■ Delivery of the strategic outputs and outcomes.

Portfolio Management

Roles	Contribution to portfolio management	Value received or delivered
Business unit (BU) and departmental managers	■ Contribute to the organisation's strategic goals ■ Have a BU perspective of contribution to the strategic goals ■ Awareness and alignment of the BU/department goals and the strategic goals ■ Actively support the portfolio processes and ways of working.	■ Unambiguous decisions ■ Follow strategic priorities to set business unit priorities.
Individual sponsors	■ Direct specific change initiatives in line with the corporate goals and strategy ■ Manage the risk in line with the portfolio risk profile ■ Ensure benefits are realised ■ Champion the portfolio management process.	■ Greater awareness of how each change initiative fits with others and the overall strategy ■ Understanding of the 'big picture' ■ Accountability to the board.
Project and programme managers	■ Manage and coordinate individual projects and change activities to contribute to the strategic goals ■ Manage the risk in line with the portfolio risk profile.	■ Increased awareness of how 'their' projects contribute to the organisation's goals and strategy ■ Consistent risk management process.

Glossary

Agile	A family of development methodologies where requirements and solutions are developed iteratively and incrementally throughout the life cycle.
Assurance	The process of providing confidence to stakeholders that projects, programmes and portfolios will achieve their objectives for beneficial change.
AXELOS, P3M3	Examples of externally available models to assess the maturity of portfolio management within an organisation. AXELOS is a joint venture company, created in 2013 by the Cabinet Office on behalf of Her Majesty's Government (HMG) in the UK and Capita plc, to manage, develop and grow the Global Best Practice Portfolio.
Balanced portfolio	A point in the portfolio life cycle where the component projects and programmes are balanced, for example, in terms of strategic alignment, overall risk, resource usage, cash flow and impact across the business. These attributes are considered in the light of data available and confidence.
Benefit	A positive and measurable impact of change.
Benefits management	The identification, definition, planning, tracking and realisation of benefits.
Benefits realisation	The practice of ensuring that benefits are derived from outputs and outcomes.
Bi-modal project management	Bi-modal project management is changing how projects are executed. Instead of having to choose one practice over another, it's about implementing more than one method across an organisation – allowing the portfolio manager to choose whichever methodology best suits each project.
Board (programme or project)	A body that provides sponsorship to a project or programme. The board will represent financial, provider and user interests.
Board (executive)	An executive body that oversees the governance of a portfolio, and provides direction on strategic goals, priorities, risk appetite and investment levels.
Business case	Provides justification for undertaking a project, programme or portfolio. It evaluates the benefit, cost and risk of alternative options and provides a rationale for the preferred solution.

Glossary

Business plans	Periodic statements of where a business unit or organisation is heading, and the actions required to achieve strategic goals and business targets. Portfolios need to be integrated and aligned with business plans in terms of investment, scope, timescales and impacts.
Business risk assessment	The assessment of risk to business objectives, rather than risk to achieving project, programme or portfolio objectives.
Business-as-usual (BAU)	An organisation's normal, day-to-day operations. Also referred to as steady-state.
C-suite	C-suite gets its name from the titles of top senior executives, whose job titles tend to start with the letter C, for chief, as in chief executive officer (CEO), chief financial officer (CFO), chief operating officer (COO), and chief information officer (CIO).
Change control	The process through which all requests to change the approved baseline of a project, programme or portfolio are captured, evaluated and then approved, rejected or deferred.
Change initiative	For this guide, any project, programme or other entity that falls within the scope of the agreed portfolio criteria.
Change management	The overarching approach taken in an organisation to move from the current to a future desirable state, using a coordinated and structured approach in collaboration with stakeholders.
Communication	The process of exchanging information and confirming there is shared understanding.
Control	Tracking performance against agreed plans and taking the corrective action required to meet defined objectives.
Context	A collective term for the governance and setting of a project, programme or portfolio.
Deliverable	A product, set of products or package of work that will be delivered to, and formally accepted by, a stakeholder.
Dependency	A relationship between activities in a network diagram; related to dependency mapping.
Environment	A collective term for the societal and/or organisational setting of a project, programme or portfolio. Also known as context.
Escalation	The process by which issues are drawn to the attention of a higher level of management.
Financial management	The process of estimating and justifying costs in order to secure funds, controlling expenditure and evaluating the outcomes.
Funding	The means by which the money required to undertake a project, programme or portfolio is secured and then made available as required.

Glossary

Governance	The framework of authority and accountability that defines and controls the outputs, outcomes and benefits from projects, programmes and portfolios. The mechanism whereby the investing organisation exerts financial and technical control over the deployment of the work and the realisation of value.
Initiative	An initiative is a set of activities or work packages that need to be completed to achieve a business objective or goal. They can be projects and/or programmes.
Investment appraisal	The analysis done to consider the profitability of an investment over the life of an asset alongside considerations of affordability and strategic fit. An input to the investment decision.
Issue	A problem that is now, or is about to, breach delegated tolerances for work on a project or programme. Issues require support from the sponsor to agree a resolution.
Leadership	The ability to establish vision and direction, to influence and align others towards a common purpose, and to empower and inspire people to achieve success.
Lessons learned	Documented experiences that can be used to improve the future management of projects, programmes and portfolios. This should be followed by an active process where new initiatives are changed in light of previous experience.
Life cycle	A framework comprising a set of distinct, high-level stages required to transform an idea or concept into reality in an orderly and efficient manner. Life cycles offer a systematic and organised way to undertake project-based work and can be viewed as the structure underpinning deployment.
Management plan	A plan that sets out how an aspect of a project, programme or portfolio will be delivered, for example a configuration management plan. Individual management plans are component parts of the overall project management plan (PMP) that is the output of integrated planning.
Management team	Those involved in the sponsorship and day-to-day management of a project, programme or portfolio.
Materiality	Materiality is a concept or convention relating to the importance or significance of an amount, transaction, or discrepancy.
MoSCoW	Acronym for 'must have', 'should have', 'could have', 'would like to have'. It is used to determine a hierarchy of, for example, requirements or benefits. If the 'must have' cannot be delivered, then the activity is not worth doing.
Objectives	A generic term for pre-determined results towards which effort is directed. Objectives may be defined in terms of outputs, outcomes and/or benefits.

Glossary

Opportunity	A positive risk event that, if it occurs, will have an upside/ beneficial effect on the achievement of one or more objectives.
Organisation	The management structure applicable to the project, programme or portfolio and the organisational environment in which it operates.
Outcome	The changed circumstances or behaviour that results from the use of an output and leads to realisation of benefits.
Output	The tangible or intangible product typically delivered by a project. Used interchangeably with deliverable and product.
Planning	Determines what is to be delivered, how much it will cost, when it will be delivered, how it will be delivered and who will carry it out.
Project (programme or portfolio) management office (PMO)	An organisational structure that provides support for projects, programmes and/or portfolios.
Portfolio	A collection of projects and/or programmes used to structure and manage investments at an organisational or functional level to optimise strategic benefits or operational efficiency.
Portfolio management	The selection, prioritisation and control of an organisation's projects and programmes, in line with its strategic objectives and capacity to deliver.
Portfolio plan	A depiction in words and diagrams of what the portfolio comprises, its major interdependencies, expected timescales and major deliverables, defining how the portfolio will be managed. Supporting analyses may include cost and benefit schedules, key risks and major stakeholders.
Portfolio risks	These would typically cover those internal and external events that will impact on the portfolio overall rather than any single project or programme. They may include such things as resource availability, implementation capacity, investment constraints and regulatory matters.
Prioritise/ prioritisation	The phase of a portfolio life cycle where priorities are set by strategic objective, return on investment (ROI) or any other chosen metric.
Product	A tangible or intangible component of a project's output. Used interchangeably with deliverable and output.
Programme	A unique, transient, strategic endeavour, undertaken to achieve beneficial change, and incorporating a group of related projects and business-as-usual (steady-state) activities.
Programme board	A body that provides sponsorship and governance to a programme. The board will represent financial, provider and user interests.
Programme management	The coordinated management of projects and business-as-usual (steady-state) activities to achieve beneficial change.
Project	A unique, transient endeavour undertaken to bring about change and to achieve planned objectives.

Glossary

Project management	The application of processes, methods, knowledge, skills and experience to achieve specific objectives for change.
Quality	The fitness for purpose or the degree of conformance of the outputs of a process, or the process itself, to requirements.
RACI	RACI is an acronym that stands for responsible, accountable, consulted and informed. A RACI chart is a matrix of all the activities or decision-making authorities undertaken in an organisation, set against all the people or roles.
Reports	(1) The presentation of information in an appropriate format (e.g. management report). (2) A written record or summary, a detailed account or statement, or a verbal account. (3) A term used to refer to a role that is subordinate to another role in an organisational structure.
Resource management	The acquisition and deployment of the internal and external resources required to deliver the project, programme or portfolio.
Resource scheduling	A collection of techniques used to calculate the resources required to deliver the work, when they will be required and what the dependencies are.
Resources	All the labour and non-labour items required to undertake the scope of work to the required quality.
Return on investment (ROI)	An expression of the value of an investment in change, based on the gain in benefit relative to the cost.
Review	A critical evaluation of a deliverable, business case or management process.
Risk	The potential of a situation or event to impact on the achievement of specific objectives.
Risk appetite	How much risk investors are willing to tolerate in achieving their objectives. Expressed as risk thresholds or tolerances.
Risk analysis and evaluation	An assessment and synthesis of risk events to gain an understanding of their individual significance and their combined impact on objectives.
Risk management	A process that allows individual risk events and overall risk to be understood and managed proactively, optimising success by minimising threats and maximising opportunities.
Risk register	A document listing identified risk events and their corresponding planned responses. Used interchangeably with risk log or risk repository.
Rolling portfolio	A portfolio that spans more than one calendar/accounting year, and which has investment funds that have not yet been allocated to specific projects or programmes, but shows how such unallocated funds align with strategic goals. It normally has a constant horizon. By their very nature, nearly all portfolios are rolling.

Glossary

Scope	The totality of the outputs, outcomes and benefits and the work required to produce them.
SMART	SMART is an acronym, giving criteria to guide in the setting of objectives, for example in project management, employee-performance management and personal development. The letters S and M mean **specific** and **measurable**. The remaining letters referring to **achievable**, **realistic** and **timely**.
Sponsor	A critical role as part of the governance board of any project, programme or portfolio. The sponsor is accountable for ensuring that the work is governed effectively and delivers the objectives that meet identified needs.
Stakeholder	Individuals or groups who have an interest or role in the project, programme or portfolio, or are impacted by it.
Stakeholder engagement	The systematic identification, analysis, planning and implementation of actions designed to influence stakeholders.
Strategic goals	Highest-level goals as set by the board of the organisation. These provide the direction and purpose for the organisation and the portfolio.
Threat	A negative risk event; a risk event that if it occurs will have a downside/detrimental effect on one or more objectives.
Users	The group of people who are intended to work with deliverables to enable beneficial change to be realised.
Vision	The future state that the portfolio is intended to deliver.
Waterfall or linear methodology	All projects, programmes and portfolios are designed to deliver objectives. These objectives may be expressed as outputs, outcomes or benefits. In a waterfall methodology, objectives are expressed in generic sequence. The most common type is a linear life cycle which is known as a waterfall method.